Minimal Motoring

from Cyclecar to Microcar

Minimal Motoring

from Cyclecar to Microcar

DAVID THIRLBY

TEMPUS

First published 2002

PUBLISHED IN THE UNITED KINGDOM BY:
Tempus Publishing Ltd
The Mill, Brimscombe Port
Stroud, Gloucestershire GL5 2QG
www.tempus-publishing.com

PUBLISHED IN THE UNITED STATES OF AMERICA BY:
Tempus Publishing Inc.
2 Cumberland Street
Charleston, SC 29401
www.tempuspublishing.com

British Library Cataloguing in Publication Data.
A catalogue record for this book is available from the British Library.

ISBN 0 7524 2367 3

Typesetting and origination by Tempus Publishing.
PRINTED AND BOUND IN GREAT BRITAIN.

Contents

Acknowledgements

Thanks are due to the many people who have helped in the writing of this book. Jacques Potherat was the man who pushed me into starting the research for this book and I, with many others, regret his early and untimely death.

I turned to the Light Car and Edwardian Section of the Vintage Sports-Car Club for advice on what I should include, since I had no desire to research every car, but to highlight the important ones such as the Bédélia, the Morgan and the GN. Bob Jones and Mike Bullett were my first mentors. They advised that it was important to have photographs of some of the oddball devices, even if they were not part of the text.

In Britain I had help from Sandy Skinner, Jon Giles, Kenneth Ball, John Warburton, David Waring, David Ridley, Peter Harper, and specifically Colin Morris and Peter Relph on the British-owned example of a Spacke. Members of the VSCC keen on French cars, such as Keith Bowley and John Blake, were also appealed to for help.

The colour picture of the Scott Sociable comes from the Bradford Industrial Museum. I am grateful to Graham Pilgrim and Gordon Fitzgerald for practically all of the post-war microcar illustrations.

I would like to thank the Veteran Car Club for allowing me to use their magnificent library and to read the American magazine *Motor Age*. C.F. Caunter wrote in the fifties about cyclecars and I read his writings published by the Science Mueum.

Two weeks in the north-eastern part of the United States of America was spent with Frank Allocca who introduced me to Dr Fred Simeone, who has an excellent collection of motoring literature and who turns out to be a key player in this book, because it was on that visit I found out about the Spacke. Also in the States I gained the co-operation of the Henry Ford Motor Museum and other chums: Tony Carroll, Dave Kimball, Lee Cowie and Doug Webb – all of whom led me down different roads of personally-uncharted cyclecar territory.

The Morgan three-wheeler was the longest lasting cyclecar and the advice, editing and co-operation from Dr Jake Alderson makes me believe that, though there may well be many errors made in this arbitrary selection of cyclecars, that the accurate one reported is the Morgan. Jake introduced Dave Pittuck and Freddie Frot from France to me, who helped on the Darmont-manufactured Morgan.

Illustrations and photographs to illustrate this volume were difficult to find. My long-standing friends John Maitland and Guy Griffiths are the main suppliers. I have been much aided by Peter Harper, who lives close by in Cheshire. Mark Joseland unearthed the photographs taken in the GN works in 1921 and Roger McDonald copied them. Tim Harding was especially helpful in finding illustrations. Those for the post-war microcars came, in the main, from Graham Pilgrim and Gordon Fitzgerald.

David Venables and John Warburton have read the story, as has my long-suffering and attractive secretary Paula Wright. The main thing that they had to search for was to try and avoid endless repetition of the same pieces of information and to eliminate non sequiturs. Thank you.

Introduction

The definition of a cyclecar and microcar used in this book is that they are simple road-going cars using, in the main, motorcycle technology. The Bédélia started the craze and the GN and Morgan followed. The Morgan three-wheeler lasted until the mid-1930s, for after that it began to use car components. The cyclecar almost disappeared in the United States of America in four short years. In Europe, the survival period was roughly from 1912 until 1923, with a further life after the end of the Second World War.

In 1909 motoring was not popular or used for business and was only indulged in by a few of two classes – the rich with big cars and the mad motorcyclist. Some cars made history and evolved with it – the prime examples being the Mercedes and the Rolls-Royce. Some made history purely in recognition of their innovation rather than their development, the Ford Model T being the best example. Other cars moulded history so that when their lifespan was over, motoring and the motor car could never be the same again, and in this category there are probably four important makes – Bugatti, Austin, Hispano-Suiza and Vauxhall.

The design of a car in 1909 for the economical niche in the market looked easy to the simple minds of Godfrey and Nash, Morgan, Borbeau (maker of the Bédélia) and a few others. Why not take a fairly powerful twin-cylinder motor-cycle engine, put it in a frame and add wheels to taste.

(Sam Clutton, Motor Sport)

The cyclecar had a short lifespan, but its influence was widespread, it led to cyclecar manufacturers setting out to make a small car with an adequate engine. The principle was that little horse-power was required, for there was very little weight to propel. The idea was taken up by most car-producing countries in the world, and it was developed in different ways according to the temperament of the countries. The cyclecar disappeared in Britain – except for the Morgan, the Raleigh and its successor the Reliant, together with the BSA three-wheelers.

Many small cars have gone well with small engines, but modern mass production and planned obsolescence was not in the minds of the cyclecar manufacturers, before or after the Great War. Nash and Godfrey were engineers, and they were only too happy to take somebody else's designs and to modify them to suit their own requirements. They were also capable – as all good engineers should be – of considering from first principles the purpose of the parts they were making. Some of their conclusions were the same as those of modern car manufacturers. Moving parts were not designed for an indefinite life; not that they deliberately planned the parts to date quickly. The one thing that separated the GN from all the other cyclecar manufacturers was the continuous product development, not only of chassis but also of engines.

The advent of American mass production methods led to ever lower prices. Morris in Britain dominated the small to middle size of car and the Austin 7 administered the *coup de grâce* for the cyclecar. The Americans built more cyclecars than any other nation in the 1914–

1917 period, but the engines were larger on the whole. It was the continuous success of the Ford Model T and its diminishing price that killed the American cyclecar.

The Morgan three-wheeler design, other than for engine and gearing changes, was the same from the beginning until the end. The GN has more than its fair share of coverage for the simple reason that the company was the wondrous exception that went in for product development – not only of engines but of chassis components as well. Hence the much greater coverage this car has in this book than any other make. The development that both Godfrey and Nash desired of cutting back production and making and selling only a sports model was not to be, but they were able to indulge themselves later – Nash with the Frazer Nash and Godfrey with the HRG.

Out of the cyclecar boom of 1918-1922 came the light French sporting cars such as the Salmson, Amilcar and Sénéchal. The French were the only nation with a logical development from the cyclecar, from the pre-1914 Bédélia and the post-1919 French-built GN, to small sports cars. These cars owed their parentage to the GN.

Formula Three racing cars of the post-war world, such as the Cooper, could fall into this cyclecar category but are felt to be outside it, as they were not designed for the open road. They are 'specific racers for a specific class'. Like many things, there are possible exceptions to this rule. Monsieur Mauve, below, in his Elfe with his one and only production model, later fitted with a tandem seat for two up could be the exceptional car but he was never a volume producer. A comparable car was the post-1945 Cooper two-seater sports with a

Monsieur Mauve in his Elfe at the 1920 Gaillon Hill Climb in France. This car is a cyclecar, but it is a racing car and falls outside the remit of this book. Monsieur Mauve only built this one car and modified it into a pillion type passenger two-seater for 1921.

"NOTHING NEW," ETC.———"Look at that, Bill; copying **us** !"

The cartoon which immortalised the Bédélia, from The Cyclecar, *December 1912.*

Triumph twin engine, which never got beyond the prototype stage. Any reader of the magazine *Iota* in April 1948 could have read of the Neve 500, designed by Kenneth Neve with a reinforced ash chassis and a flat twin Douglas 500cc engine, and felt that cyclecars were alive and well; the Neve 500 was competing at the time of the beginning of the Cooper 500 dominance.

The European countries revived their interest and became cyclecar-conscious in the post-war period, though avoiding the term cyclecar. The word 'microcar' came into use. This revival was due entirely to the same reasoning as had been the driving force in 1910 and 1919, that of the need for low price and economy in operation.

The three-wheeler was found attractive due to favourable tax regulations. Designers after the Second World War re-examined the possibilities, since there were so many components that could be bought and assembled into a motor car and with minimum development into a sporting car. This had been exactly the drive that set Borbeau, Godfrey and Nash with Morgan on their way.

No attempt has been made to include all cyclecar manufacturers in this slim volume; the aim is primarily to draw a picture of the changing times. Post Second World War there was a resurgence across the world, except for America, in cheap, simple motoring. These vehicles were given the grander name, however, of 'microcar'.

1
The Life of the Cyclecar

The tricar seemed to be the future for low-powered and economical private transportation at the turn of the century, and for the few years between 1905 and 1909. The motor tricar, a three-wheeled device with the engine and transmission behind the driver and passenger, was an inadequate compromise between the motorcycle and the motor car. At its crudest it was a motorcycle with a two-wheel appendage in front of the main chassis frame and was the basis of innumerable cheaply produced lightweight delivery vans. Two people could sit side by side at the very front between the two wheels with the smelly, noisy engine behind them. In Britain the Riley and AC were the major manufacturers, but there were many others building some cars and hopeful of success.

The voiturette, a scaled-down large car with an engine, radiator and bonnet in front of the driver, was the future. There were also two new and advanced forms of light motor vehicle – the cyclecar and the light car, which were both under development in many countries.

A.C. Arthur Armstrong in his 1946 book *Bouverie Street to Bowling Green Lane*, the history of the Temple Press publishing house, stated that there were two widely held beliefs of the first decade of the century. Firstly, that the motorcycle was doomed and, secondly, that motorcycle sport did not have a future worthy of consideration.

The Chater Lea Carette of 1907 was a precursor of the cyclecar, fitted with a vee twin Sarolea engine and single belt final drive.

By 1910, motor cars and motorcycles had evolved from their primitive stages of development into vehicles which were close to providing reliable transport. The engines for light cars were simplistic, having been designed and made to the motorcycle standards of the time. Most of the cars or devices offered on sale were built up from proprietary offerings. Ignition systems, if not reliable, were moving towards that state; practical spray carburettors were in production, and gearboxes and clutches were effective. Refinements such as electric lighting, mechanical and electric engine-starting systems and shock absorber devices were still in the future, but becoming available in America.

Many individuals, unknown to each other, and in many countries, were working towards the same end of producing a car using motorcycle and off-the-shelf technology, with no particular plans for going into the business of manufacture. These were do-it-yourself backyard enterprises for the personal amusement of the constructors. It was only after the passage of two or three years that these pioneers realised that they had created an entirely new movement within the growing motor industry and drew together to follow the common path. In 1909 the two favoured names for these lightweight cars were 'monocar' and 'duocar'.

In France there were two active enthusiasts, L.F. de Peyrecave and Robert Bourbeau, and it was the latter with his friend, Henri Devaux, who triggered off the cyclecar vogue. 'One-off job designs' were appearing on the roads in Britain, and the Temple Press journal *Motor Cycling* became interested in what appeared to be a development in their sphere, but whether it was really a new kind of motorcycle with four wheels or a light car with a motorcycle engine was something that caused the Editor, W.G. McMinnies, to think about the future.

It was said at the time that if there were two Germans marooned on an island, within a week they would have produced a new philosophy, two Frenchmen a duel and two Englishmen a club. Indeed, the untranslatable word 'club' has been given by the British to the world, like the French terms chassis and chauffeur. The rest of Europe and the world absorbed the word 'club' from the very beginnings of motoring. The first motor club of all was formed out of enthusiasm for the new sport of motor racing. In 1894 the historic first motor run took place from Paris to Rouen, and the following year the Automobile Club de France was founded. Two years later Britain hailed the birth of the Automobile Club of Great Britain and Ireland, which became the Royal Automobile Club in 1907. Regional motor clubs followed quickly. The Midland Automobile Club ran its first hill-climb in 1901 and at Shelsley Walsh in 1905. A joint Committee of the Royal Automobile Club and the Auto-Cycle Union, which was convened in the spring of 1912, considered the new form of light motor car. It was decided that the generic name should be a 'cyclecar'. That same year, motoring had its first club dedicated to the development and enjoyment of a new kind of motor car with the foundation of the Cyclecar Club.

In 1902 one of the founders of the Motor Cycling Club, the largest and most active club in the country, was Ernest Penman, once a racing cyclist who had joined Temple Press to launch *Cycling* and became general manager. Waylaying a harassed Armstrong, he put the suggestion to him of a cyclecar magazine, and found it instantly snapped up. The *Cyclecar* staff operated in an office in the Temple Press Rosebery Avenue premises, where they worked to prepare the first issue of the journal. By 1912 the cyclecar movement was booming. Companies were being formed all over the country and there was furious hammering and welding to prepare models for the forthcoming October Motor Cycle Show. A meeting was assembled for a round table exploratory discussion where, among others, were Frank 'Hippopo' Thomas, Osmond Hill, H.R. Godfrey, Glynn Rowden, W.G. McMinnies and

Armstrong in the chair. The upshot was the decision to call an open meeting in London, at the Holborn Restaurant, on 30 October.

There were about sixty present that Wednesday evening in the Edwardian glories of the famous old restaurant which stood at the corner of Kingsway and Holborn. Into the chair they voted Revd E.P. Greenhill, who was chairman of the Competitions Committee of the ACU. At this stage in the development of motoring the motorcycling people regarded cyclecarism as a branch of their own activities. The RAC, on the other hand, was dubious about admitting the new machines to the dignified car world. When everybody had settled down, C.S. Burney (of Burney & Blackburne, makers of motorcycle engines with the outside flywheel) proposed that a club be formed, seconded by F.A. McNab. The proposal was accepted and officers had been appointed at the Motor Cycle Show at Olympia, on 29 November: W.G. McMinnies was proposed as the Club Captain; Frank 'Hippopo' Thomas as Hon. Secretary; A.C. Armstrong agreed to become the Treasurer; and Glynn Rowden was nominated as Club Chairman. A Rules Committee was appointed: H.P. White; W. Cooper; F.A. McNab; E. Hapgood; D. Kapadia; Revd E.P. Greenhill; Dr A.M. Low, a scientist whose enthusiasm for anything new and progressive knew no bounds; E.M.P. Boileau; E.H. Taylor; R.M. Stallbrass; A.E.Parnacott; A.W. Ayden; R.W. George; R. Cleave; Glynn Rowden; A.C. Armstrong; F.S. Whitworth; Percy Bradley; G.N. Higgs; F.C. Whitworth; E.C. Paskell; R. Surridge; R.F. Messervy; A. Selwyn; Osmond Hill; Archie Nash; W.G. McMinnies; Maj. Lindsay Lloyd; Laurie Cade, the Fleet Street journalist; Gambier Weeks; J.N. Barrett, C.S. Burney and F.L. Goodacre – a number of leading cycle-carists who managed to produce a set of rules within a month.

The inaugural meeting duly took place at Olympia with Glynn Rowden in the chair. Business was brisk. The subscription was fixed at one guinea with half a guinea for country members and for ladies. The proposed officers were elected en bloc and Osmond Hill agreed to help Thomas as the Assistant Hon. Secretary. Between fifty and sixty people joined there and then.

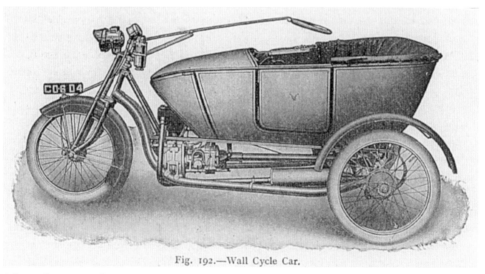

Fig. 192.—Wall Cycle Car.

The Wall Tri-car, made in Birmingham 1911, had a single or twin-cylinder engine and the transmission was by a Roc clutch and two-speed epicyclic gearbox.

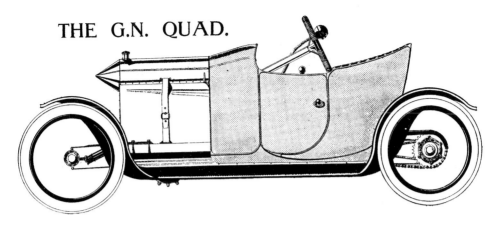

THE G.N. QUAD.

The GN Quad of 1912, standing for quadricar, before the term cyclecar came into use.

All was not sweetness and light, however, for there was one man who challenged every rule as it was proposed, criticised everything, further he demanded that no one in the trade should be admitted to membership and, having departed that night, was never heard of again.

The first outing was reported:

A motor-bus turned round to look at us. Taxicabs thought they should give way, sidling down to the kerb in their best Saturday morning style. A pair of equine thoroughbreds stood upon their hind legs and pawed the air with delight. A tram driver pulled up his house-on-wheels with such a jerk that the passengers were shot on the floor. A portly pedestrian, making his fourth attempt to cross Piccadilly Circus, bathed in the mud instead. Even the man on point duty put an electric-light standard between himself and the peril of the streets. And then we passed.

The roar of the 8hp JAP swept up the torrent of abuse that marked our passage as we churned through a sea of slimy, yellow mud that made the heart of the stoutest taxicab driver turn faint. Not so the heart of our Duocar as we rocketed over the greasiest streets of south-east London. Beyond Putney we picked up a GN and, as one cyclecarist to another, hooted merrily, trod on the accelerator pedal and gave the glad-eye for a speed exhibition up Putney Hill. The GN, being in the hands of some reckless young fellow, won easily, and we considered, as we picked up various cars one by one, that their drivers were not looking too pleased about it. Later on, the GN enthusiasts were discovered warming their hands by the roadside. So, hastily referring them to The Cyclecar Manual and giving a nod to three gloomy-looking gentlemen in charge of a 'measured furlong', we made Kingston, Ditton and Esher without incident.

At Esher, the GN came roaring by triumphantly. At 'The Bear', a Duo-ist was observed taking in 'home fuel'. Presently, he too came to the front to give us an exhibition of skilful driving, which we took to be a display of figure skating.

At Wisley Hut there were already half a dozen arrivals, besides an equal number of motor-carists, who gathered round to gaze, awe-struck, at slackened belts resting in the mud.

'Aren't they awful?' said one. 'How they drive with belts hitting the ground beats me.' We informed him that we'd had the wind behind. Every few minutes another arrival would perform the customary finishing sprint and brake test, until there were nearly two dozen machines lined

up at the roadside. These included five Duos, three GNs, three Humberettes, two GWKs, Parnacott's quaint looking iron-clad, an AC Sociable, an Autotrix, an Averies, a Sherwin, and a Bédélia, besides several of the homemade variety.

Had there been an 'appearance prize', it would have been divided between Higgs (whose beautiful lilac-hued GN was almost spotless, thanks to a neat arrangement of auxiliary wings) and the passenger who had been used as a mud shield on an experimental Duo, the front or the back of whose head could only be made out by his overcoat buttons.

Some thirty members and friends sat down to lunch in an apparently very subdued frame of mind, for was this not a very sedate and historic occasion? Only one lady member (there are two altogether) was present. Having been disappointed in the delivery of a new cyclecar, she had cycled down to the run.

After lunch, half the party followed the Revd E.P. Greenhill's GWK over the Surrey hills, in response to his invitation to take tea with him at Walton-on-the-Hill. Up, up, through winding lanes we sped, Thomas's big GN 'Hippopo-Thomas', scattering mud forty feet behind it, and drowning all remonstrance with a bark that could be heard for ten miles. Keeping discreetly out of range, we had a wonderful vista of a long procession of the low-built, rakish-looking cars winding over the hills. Every now and then a dip in the road would shut out a view of the procession and then, far off, we would espy it once more, speeding swiftly up the opposite slope.

A driving mist of rain swept across the country, but what cared we as we tore over squelching roads with the crackle of a score of exhausts in front to guide our way and promise company at the journey's end? The spiritual joy of the new motoring makes light of fleshly ills. It was dusk when we pulled up and joined the thronged tea tables.

'Our last glimpse of the first run of the Cyclecar Club was of 'Hippopo-Thomas' roaring through the night, silhouetted against the wide arc of its searchlight. Suddenly, 'Hippopo-Thomas' threw up its back wheels and disappeared from view! It had shot clean across the main road and into the ditch on the far side! Fortunately, it does not require a crane to haul a cyclecar out of difficulties, and two lusty cyclecarists made light work of pushing 'Hippopo-Thomas' back on to the road again. We let the big GN light the way, keeping to the sodden road with difficulty, speeding north and homewards through streaming rain, damp, happy, and thrilled with the joy of a wild, cross-country drive.

The first all-cyclecar trial was held that same month, by the Sutton Coldfield Automobile Club on a 100-mile circuit out to Stratford-on-Avon and Buckinghamshire, at the conclusion of which eight gold medals were awarded to: Rex Mundy, GWK, he was later competitions manager to the KLG company; G. Bryant, Motorette three-wheeler; P.J. Evans, Humberette; E.R. Wintle, Rollo tandem; A.G. Eames, A.C. Sociable; H.F. S. Morgan, Morgan; B.W. Bailey, Crescent; and F.H. Stevenson, Morgan. L.F. de Peyrecave had exchanged his first love of a Bédélia for the English Duo.

As soon as it became known that the new journal was in preparation and as more and more vehicles were coming onto the roads, the Auto-Cycle Union decided to adopt the new machines under its wing, rather than allow the RAC to gain control and have the membership fees. A conclave was therefore duly assembled at the RAC premises, under the chairmanship of Col. H.C. L. Holden, who had supervised the plans for the building of Brooklands a few years earlier. Col. Lindsay Lloyd, Clerk of the Course at Brooklands and an ACU committee member, came up with the suggestion for the new cars of 'cyclecar', which was immediately adopted. McMinnies was to be the first editor. On 27 November 1912, *The*

Archie Nash, with Ron Godfrey beside him, leads an AC with J. Mundy in a 1912 Brooklands race.

Archie Nash at the wheel with Ron Godfrey and the interim GN engine design of a JAP with Peugeot barrels, the crankcase was soon replaced with the GN ninety-degree bottom end.

A GWK of 1912 period ready for the war.

Cyclecar was on sale for a penny – it had sixty-four pages plus a further eighty-four pages of advertisements, and measured 11in by 8in. Over 100,000 copies were sold to the amazement of the trade and the satisfaction of the sponsors.

Edward Dangerfield, the managing director of Temple Press, had inserted an opinion in the first issue of *Cyclecar* that 'despite a contrary opinion very generally expressed by motor manufacturers and others, we predict that, in the not very distant future, there will be an intense demand for the four wheeled single seater.' As Arthur Armstrong recorded in 1946 – 'the prediction has yet to be fulfilled.'

On 14 December 1912 at a meeting of the Fédération Internationale des Clubs Moto Cycliste, it was formally decided that there should be an international classification of cyclecars to be accepted by England, Canada, the United States, France, Holland, Belgium, Italy, Austria and Germany.

It was decided to establish two classes of cyclecars, as follows:

    (i) Large class

Maximum weight	772lb
Maximum engine capacity	1,100cc
Minimum tyre section	60mm

   (ii) Small class

Minimum weight	330lb
Maximum weight	660lb
Maximum enginecapacity	750cc
Minimum tyre section	55mm

The cyclecar, with economy as its chief feature, was optimistically hailed as 'the new motoring'. A cyclecar was described at the time as a combination of the worst characteristics

THE
Largest Selection
of
CYCLECARS
at

Harrods

A.C.	Bayard	Humberette	Metz	Peugeot (Baby)	Swift
Autorette	C.L.C.	L.E.C.	Morgan	Phanomobile	Violette
Averies	G.W.K.	Motorette	Premier	Singer	Warne

 # THE PREMIER HOUSE
FOR DEFERRED PAYMENTS

ONLY 2½ % EXTRA.

EXAMPLE—
You can buy a cyclecar costing £125 for a first payment
of only £32 - 2 - 6 and 12 monthly payments of £8 - 0 - 0

WRITE FOR HARRODS CYCLECAR LIST.

HARRODS L^{TD} RICHARD BURBIDGE MANAGING DIRECTOR LONDON·S·W

Telephone No.—Western One '80 lines).
Telegrams—"Everything, Earrods, London."

A Harrods of Knightsbridge advertisement of November 1912. Harrods could never be thought of as a motor trading emporium. But for a brief period they, as so many people, thought that the cyclecar was the new motoring and here to stay.

of a motorcycle and the more depressing features of a motor car. All cyclecars had to have clutches and change-speed gears. Simply and with very little cost, this could be managed by slipping the belt on the pulley and then varying the pulley diameter to change the gear ratio.

Harold E. Dew, a founder club member of the Cyclecar Club, was at the Holborn Restaurant meeting. He was but one of many who came into the movement by building his own machine in 1910, with the idea of constructing a vehicle to cost about £35. Unfortunately, he must have miscalculated something because he had spent £100 before he started putting the parts together. He ended up with a central box-type chassis, which he straddled like a motor-cycle, but, though it had no bodywork of any description, it had an engine and four wheels. In his enthusiasm he let it be known that he was prepared to help others with design and fabrication. In eight weeks he had over 300 replies – one asking how much he would charge for a batch of a dozen.

Fritz Sabell, builder of the Sabella, began in an even simpler manner, although he was making light cars in 1906. His first contrivance had no engine, and was propelled by the occupant wrenching away at a hand lever working a driving chain by a ratchet and a free wheel. In a moment of frenzy he designed a six-seater, in which all six occupants (they could hardly be termed passengers) were to row themselves along with six levers. The single-seat prototype worked, for Sabell was accustomed to row himself around the district before breakfast, but he capitulated to fit a small engine and was in serious business. Sabell was to become the English agent for Bédélia.

One of the earliest British designs was the Rollo with its Zenith Gradua variable drive pulleys, which provided the clutch when the belts were slackened off. The Rollo had taken a leaf out of the Bédélia book, with its tandem seating and rear seat steering, though the later Rollo models had front seat steering. The Rollo had disappeared by 1914, even though it had been promoted as having the advantages of a motorcycle and a motor car – combining the luxury and safety of one and the economies of the other. The Rollo sales brochure was very dismissive of sidecar outfits – 'that wicker-work monstrosity – a pram attached to a bicycle'.

A Sabella of 1912.

The "Rollo-Sociable"

PRICE:

95 Guineas
READY FOR THE ROAD.

100 Guineas
WITH ADJUSTABLE WIND
SCREEN AND HOOD.

SPECIFICATION:

As Standard, but
STEERING rigid
Ackermann type,
Suspension Rear
Wheels, semi-
elliptical springs.
Front Wheels
— sprung —
independently

The Rollo had a loyal group of owners, but the company only lasted from 1913 until 1914.

The cyclecar entrepreneurs, who were mostly young and working in small workshops, soon disappeared under economic stress. Some firms that existed were building light cars purporting to be cyclecars that were not light enough for enthusiasts. Cyclecar enthusiasts saw that something no heavier and not more costly to buy or run than a motorcycle and sidecar was the requirement.

Single-cylinder powered cars with De Dion or JAP engines had no prospects. The simple V-twin air-cooled motorcycle engine, frequently of proprietary brands, like JAP, Coventry-Simplex, Precision with the Swiss-built MAG, were in the majority, but there were others. LEC went so far as to use a water-cooled twin. Alldays had a water-cooled single.

It was preferred to set the engine at right angles to the drive, although the simplest method was to fit it like a motorcycle, fore and aft, and take off the drive by chain to a countershaft. Cylinders at a ninety degree angle produced the best balance and smoothest running. Singer & Wilkinson went so far as to fit four-cylinder water-cooled engines, at which the purists raised scornful eyebrows and muttered about disguised light cars for the rich. There was a press story of an advanced form of two-stroke, with a piston-type pump to blow pure air through the combustion chamber to scavenge the burnt charge before a valve admitted the next firing charge, but nothing else was ever reported of this engine.

One of the oddest examples of what now seem a pretty odd collection at the Olympia exhibition of 1912 was the Wall which looked like a motorcycle with sidecar chassis, on which was perched a two-seater bath tub known as a 'sociable'. The driver steered by means of a long tiller attached to the front wheel forks where the handlebars should have been. Transmission was by shaft to a proper differential. It was priced 'from 90 guineas'. The Scott Sociable and the Seal, in which the 'sociable' bath tub was alongside the motorcycle component, looked bizarre and an obvious compromise and were destined for a short life.

During the first winter of the Cyclecar Club's existence, Dr A.M. Low, who was to serve as a valued adviser to motoring club councils for many years, delivered a lecture at the Institution of Mechanical Engineers in London, during which he cheerfully demonstrated a method of transmitting a half tone picture by radio, a good ten years before it became standard practice in Fleet Street. This remarkable man, whose after dinner speeches were a feature of Club gatherings for forty years, was ready to explain the phenomenon of the whirring of an insect's wings, the inherent inefficiency of a petrol engine or the increase in weight of a building when a butterfly alighted on its eaves, would at the drop of a hat with the most engaging urbanity, deliver a speech and his stories were what was known at the time as 'racy'. He was a high-level advocate of the new motoring – the cyclecar.

The first Cyclecar Club Trial of 1912 had the following drivers and cars competing: J. Munday, AC; K. Kreitmeyer, Zebra; A.C. Armstrong, GN; H.R. Godfrey, GN; J.T. Wood, GWK; W. Wilkinson, GWK; V. Wilberforce, GWK; H.F. S. Morgan, Morgan; Vernon Busby, Morgan; A.W. Lambert, Morgan; J.W. Spencer, Morgan; J. Averies, Averies; A. Percy Bradley, Duo; L.F. de Peyrecave, Duo; L. Cass, Gordon; W. Cooper, Humberette; Bamford, Humberette; Capt. H. Clark, Invicta; and Lionel Martin, Singer.

It was the inventors of the three separate cyclecars – the Bédélia, the Morgan and GN – who were the heralds of the future. The motor tricar formula was carried forward by the AC as it was thought that it might well produce an important car. The Humberette, according to the column inches expended on the design in the British motoring press, was assured to become a motor car, however it was not to be.

This new form of light and economical motor car, the cyclecar, could at about a penny a mile, transport one or two people in moderate comfort and at fairly high average speeds over long distances. The concept quickly found favour among a now rapidly growing motoring and motorcycling public. In 1911 there were less than a dozen different makers of cyclecars

Tom, L.T.C. Rolt, captioned this picture in his book Motoring, 'One can imagine pleading to be left to die in peace rather than face being borne away in this fashion on a Bédélia cyclecar.'

Lining up for the start of the 1913 Amiens Cyclecar GP. Number 20 is Esser in a Mathis; beside Esser is probably Leveque in a Super; the row in front has Douglas Hawkes in the Dew converted into a two-seater; 17 is Violet in the Violet-Bogey; the driver of number 11 is a sidecarist chatting to Archie Nash with the GN 18; the row in front is Borbeau in his Bédélia; 'Snowy' Whitehead's GN and 15 is Messervy with a Duocar. In front of them are the three-wheelers and sidecar outfits that started first in the race.

in Britain, and the same number in France, while there were none in the United States. By 1914, there were well over a hundred different makers of cyclecars in each of these countries, as well as others in Germany, Austria and other European countries. These designs, many produced in handful quantities only, employed varying arrangements of wheels, seating accommodation, and engine and transmission systems; they ranged in general from the simplest open construction with a single-cylinder engine to a multi-cylinder car in miniature. Prices varied from £60 to £200.

The Cyclecar Movement, or New Motoring, contained many elements of a radical political party. Revolutionary both in ideas and ideology, fervent in its adherents who were impervious either to criticism or vicissitude, it was anti-establishment and even left-wing. Yet it was always sociable in its aims rather than political. *The Cyclecar* and *The American Cyclecar* magazines, having harnessed the latent enthusiasm of the 'New Motorists', proceeded to exert proprietorial influences over the whole cyclecar movement. The doctrine advocated a purity and simplicity in the designs of the cyclecar, but also to an extent in the lives of the cyclecarists. In the beginning, at least, the accent was upon the romance of the open road, the family outing in the healthy open air, the picnic, the fun of it all.

By 1913, and with the smack of temperance fervour, *The Cyclecar* was propounding its ideas for 'The Simple Life Hotel', where the fare was to be plain but good, the charges moderate, and the rooms clean and comfortable. Owners of 40/50hp Rolls-Royces or 'gilded youths driving snorting Mercs' would most definitely not be catered for, but 'Followers of the New Motoring' on a modest cyclecar tour would be made welcome with a 5*s* six course dinner and a 3*s* 6*d* lunch!

The credit for producing the first true cyclecar has been rightly given to Robert Bourbeau of Paris who, early in 1910, produced a light, long-wheel-based cyclecar, the Bédélia, with two seats arranged in tandem – the driver's seat being located over the rear axle. He was advised before producing the car that the French road taxation would classify tandem seating as a motorcycle with evident savings. An 8hp twin-cylinder air-cooled motorcycle engine was situated in front and drove a countershaft by chain; the final drive to the rear wheels was effected by two long V-section belts running over pulleys. A clutch action was obtained by arranging for the rear axle to be moved slightly backwards or forwards by means of a hand control, thus tightening or slackening the belt tension. In addition, moving the rear axle forward still further brought the belt pulleys on the wheels against fixed shoes for braking purposes, in the manner used by Léon Bollée in his 1896 tricar. The addition of two-diameter driving pulleys, in conjunction with the forward movement of the rear wheel, provided a variation in gear ratio. This was achieved by using a piece of timber to flick the belt over to the other ratio on both sides of the car. If a passenger was being carried then he could carry this operation out, whilst the driver observed the road. The availability of the Zenith Gradua variable vee-drive from the United States modernised the gear changing procedure of the Bédélia. The track was only 3ft wide, without a differential, and the steering was by means of wire cables and pulleys which controlled a centrally-pivoted front axle. The weight of the vehicle was less than 400lb.

The Bédélia cyclecar had some success for years, both on the Continent and in French export markets for touring, commercial and racing purposes. The most glaring disadvantage of the design was the absence of Ackermann steering, but the Bédélia was stable and steerable because of its long wheelbase. The first public appearance of the car was over a course of 138 miles, which it covered at an average speed of 38mph; its maximum speed on the track was 55mph. This design continued in production for some years and coped with the order book increase, through further funding by the Potherat family. Bédélia survived under different management after the First World War until 1925, though none of the later post-1921 cars survive. In fact there may have only been prototypes made in 1921.

Monsieur Noël in a Noël at Amiens in 1913.

Borbeau stands behind the successful Bédélia at Amiens in 1913.

A number of other designs appeared in France which followed the Bédélia, such as the Automobilette and the Super. The former was a more compact version of the Bédélia, with side-by-side seating, and a smoother body line; the latter was arranged with tandem seats, the driver's seat being located in front. Both the Bédélia and the Automobilette had the same drives and steering. The long body space of these vehicles provided a large carrying capacity, and some single-seat forms were arranged as commercial delivery vans. The stretcher-carrying variant used by the French army in the First World War was a news editor's dream, with the stretcher case laid and strapped down along the bonnet. The weight of these cars was about 400-500lb.

Contemporary with the Bédélia, the GN cyclecar was produced in England by H.R. Godfrey and A.G.F. Nash. The initial 'F' in Nash's name stood for Frazer and when, in 1923, he set up his own in business, making the Frazer Nash car, he used the surname of Frazer Nash (but for the purposes of this book he is A.G.F. Nash). After the war, when he had obtained a commission in the RAF, he was widely known as Capt. Nash, or as just plain Archie Nash.

The important feature of the GN, after the first year of prototyping, was the ninety-degree vee-twin engine which was designed by the partners especially for cyclecar use. The vee-twin had a capacity of 984cc (80mm by 98mm), with automatic inlet valves located over mechanically-operated exhaust valves; a year later the inlet valves were mechanically operated by means of push rods and rockers. A single-throw crankshaft was carried in a long plain bearing, and a heavy external flywheel was used and a fan assisted cooling. With this improved engine, which made possible a top speed of about 45mph, the GN cyclecar became a practical vehicle.

The decision by the FIM (the International Federation for motor cycling) to fix a maximum engine size of 1,100cc capacity for the cyclecar engine, was the impetus to the increase of the GN engine capacity to 1,087cc (84mm by 98mm). It was the Cyclecar Grand Prix at Amiens of 1913 that was the greater impetus to refine and make the GN an important

A 1914 D'Ultra. Made by Harold Dew, maker of the Dewcar, with a Chater-Lea engine and friction transmission.

make and the Grand Prix GN, for so the production model produced was named, was capable of 60mph. Neither of the two GNs finished the race. The Amiens race was dominated by the Morgan three-wheeler driven by McMinnies which finished first, but was promptly disallowed by the French as they determined, after the race, that the event was for four-wheeled devices with an entirely separate class for three-wheelers. The British celebrated the Morgan victory, but the French stated that a Bédélia had won.

The 1913-1914 GNs, which were described as racing or sports models with a reinforced ash chassis, had four chains providing two or three forward speeds and reverse, or four forward speeds. During the 1913-1914 period Godfrey and Nash had come to the conclusion that motor racing attracted buyers and that higher specification models were more readily sold. They commenced the building of two special high-performance models, known as the single-seater racer 'Kim' and the two-seater sports racer 'Bluebottle', both cars had the same engine with various advanced features of bronze cylinder heads with inclined overhead valves of large diameter, a hemispherical combustion chamber, and ball bearings for the support of the external supported crankshaft. This engine developed 30hp at 3,400rpm, and gave the single-seater Kim GN cyclecar a maximum speed of 80mph.

A new works was built at Hendon in 1913, and the following year production started with two cars a week. The improved Grand Prix model and a simple touring model, to sell at 88 guineas, were scheduled for 1915. Production stopped during the war, and the only car work carried out during that time was the design and building of the chain-driven prototype that was to become the post-war model. The two-seater model, which was being designed for the 1914 Cyclecar Grand Prix, had a developed standard engine with deep cylinder fins, and was capable of 55mph. It was the intention of the partners to take to the 1914 Cyclecar Grand Prix at Amiens a spare engine, which would be to a Kim specification, if the French had developed racing engines for their entries.

A 1915 Gillyard fitted with an 8hp Chater-Lea engine.

Many cyclecars were constructed as one-offs by individuals. Mr John Perry built this three-wheeler with a Precision engine and a four-speed gearbox with final belt drive in 1915. The suspension was by coil springs at the front with wire and bobbin steering.

There was also the Buckingham, which before the war looked as if it had a future. The chain-cum-belt driven cyclecars produced by J.F. Buckingham from 1912 were fitted with proprietary Precision overhead-valve air-cooled (746cc) single and (1,095cc) vee-twin cylinder engines; two primary chain drives running on different ratio sprockets provided two speeds with individual cone clutches coupling the selected chain to a cross shaft. The final drive to the rear wheels was taken through two external vee-belts running on pulleys on the cross shaft. The vee-twin cylinder engines had their cylinders set at ninety degrees to each other as did the GN, and were therefore better balanced than the majority of other vee-twin cylinder engines of this period, which had fifty or sixty degree, included angle cylinders.

Most of the simpler cyclecars were not fitted with reverse gears in the interests of simplicity, together with lower manufacturing costs, since they were light enough to be pushed backwards. Later Buckingham cyclecars had a reverse gear, which was operated through a separate primary vee-belt.

Various designers were taken with the notion that men with families might look favourably on a car that was similar in concept to a motorcycle and sidecar combination. The Scott Sociable and the Seal are the prime examples in Britain, though the Sinclair Militor in the States was a very advanced design using a single steel pressing as the main structure. Alfred Scott had, by 1923, improved the design of his triangulated chassis with the engine, which had a hand starting handle operated from inside the car. The handle now turned the engine over twice with a single pull. Creature comforts were a major consideration in the design and mudguards which were integral in the body, also incorporated arm rests on the inside. To many people it looked like a car with one front wheel missing and was considered quite bizarre.

Violet, sister-in-law of Alfred Scott, with AS 154 (Scott had many vehicles with the AS registration). She used to advise Alfred on colours and was responsible for the Scott purple. Alfred, like ten per cent of all men, suffered from a level of colour blindness. This is an early Scott Sociable, probably 1914, with a single headlight and a vee slit in the windscreen, since there was no wiper for the early models.

The 1924 Scott Sociable as illustrated in the catalogue as issued by the Scott Autocar Co. of Lidgett Green, Bradford in Yorkshire, founded in 1919. The two headlights instead of one were a development for this £135 car, originally on the market for the grander 250 guineas.

Other designs that were launched which employed a 7-9hp Precision air-cooled engine, utilising motorcycle assemblies, tended to have a short life, since the margins for the assembler were financially constricted. The Armstrong-Triplex three-speed motorcycle epicyclic hub gear, with a multi-plate clutch was fitted to a number of designs. This unit was arranged in the chassis as a countershaft gear, to which the engine drove through a primary vee-belt and a secondary chain to the rear axle. The Cumbria, fitted with an 8-10 JAP engine, employed a three-speed Sturmey-Archer motorcycle hub-gear in the same manner. Another example of the cyclecar epicyclic gear was the American Spacke two-speed, clutch and reverse unit. This unit contained two epicyclic-gear trains operated by individual contracting-brake bands; in top gear the whole unit was locked solid, and the operation of either gear train provided a low gear or a reverse gear. Like the later Trojan such an arrangement meant that in an emergency the gear lever could be thrust into first, or even reverse, to provide, with a certain amount of smoke, exemplary stopping power. It was obvious in 1914 that various American companies were about to launch a range of cyclecars, but with the low price of petrol in the States and the winning formula of the Ford T type motor car being produced in epic numbers and at a steadily reducing sales price, it was difficult to see how the cyclecar could ever be a success in the United States.

Chain-cum-belt or the all-chain driven cyclecar was the most favoured transmission for the cheaper designs. Among the many types that appeared before 1914 was the Globe, which used a flat primary belt. Vee-belts were the normal drive for cars such as the Adamson, Victor, Duo, Gillyard, Gordon, JAR, LM, Sabella, Winter, Warne and Ranger built in Britain; the Hurlin, and CID in France; and the Pioneer, Falcon, Malcolm, Imp, Scripps-Booth and Ranger in the USA. Many of these designs used the tandem configuration for seating which followed the design concept of the Bédélia and used the lone or double vee-belt secondary drive to minimise belt wear and improve belt grip on the small diameter driving pulleys.

The Morgan

In 1910, there appeared the prototype of the most successful cyclecar – the three-wheeled machine produced by H.F.S. Morgan. To some extent it was derivative of the earlier tricar type, but it also had features which made it a unique and highly successful design. A bevel gear box with its cross shaft and two secondary chain drives, providing two forward gear ratios which were selected by dog clutches, transmitted the power to the sprung rear wheel. A simple fixed axle held the two steerable front wheels through the medium of independent coil springs and hence the car was fitted from its very beginning with independent front wheel suspension. This prototype Morgan cyclecar embodied the essential features upon which all Morgan three-wheelers produced during the following forty years were based. Fitted with a single bucket seat, foot-boards and tiller-steering, it made its first appearance as a 'runabout' at the Olympia Show of 1910. A chassis demonstrated the design features. The qualities of economy, compactness and good performance were quickly developed into a complete cyclecar, with a side-by-side body, and a more powerful vee-twin-cylinder engines. The fact that it was taxed at a lower rate than a four-wheeled car was a powerful incentive to purchase – it had to stay within the 8cwt bracket to meet this low tax position in the market.

All later production models had an enclosed two-seat side-by-side body, the engine was enclosed in a bonnet, a steering wheel and a gearbox to make the steering less savagely direct was substituted for the original tiller steering, and a windscreen and hood could be fitted as extras.

A variety of body styles became available by 1913, including the two-seat tourer, the 'Grand-Prix' named after the 1913 Amiens race, the 'Aero' and also the four-seat tourer. vee-twin cylinder air and water-cooled JAP engines of 996cc capacity were fitted, but other units of the same general type were also used, including the MAG, Precision and Green designs. The Morgan three-wheeler in addition to proving itself an excellent touring cyclecar, as was shown by its successes in long distance trials such as the London–Edinburgh and London–Exeter. It was also very successful in sprint races, hill climbs and track and road racing. In December 1912, H.F.S. Morgan established a cyclecar record by covering nearly sixty miles in an hour at Brooklands, for which he gained the Cyclecar Trophy. The Morgan continued in favour for some forty years, with about 20,000 being built.

Friction Drive

An alternative system of transmission was friction drive because of its simplicity. The most successful and popular of the friction-driven cyclecars which were produced, was the GWK, produced by Messrs Grice, Wood & Keiller in 1911. The GWK was acceptable to the hierarchy of the new cyclecar movement even though the cars weighed at least 2cwt more than say the GN. This form of friction-drive construction provided the maximum flexibility of operation with the minimum complexity of construction, and so long as it was driven intelligently it was a reliable and practical vehicle. The face of the external flywheel served as a friction-driving disc; across which the periphery of a driven fabric-edged disc could be moved along the splines on the shaft, upon which it was mounted. This shaft was flexibly supported so that the fabric disc could be pressed against or released from the face of the

A 1917 GWK was more of a light car than a cyclecar, but was acceptable to the Cyclecar Club.

flywheel for the purpose of increasing or decreasing the friction between the two members. The moving of the driven disc across one side of the flywheel face varied the forward gear ratio, while moving it across the centre to the other side of the face provided a reverse rotation. The driven shaft was coupled with the live rear axle.

This simple transmission arrangement was effective, although care and skill was necessary, particularly in the application of the drive through the friction surfaces. Any harshness which caused the flywheel face to revolve for an undue length of time against the stationary periphery of the driven wheel tended to wear flats in the fabric of the latter, resulted in a rough and unreliable drive. With careful use, the friction rim would cover some 5,000 miles without trouble before renewal was required as a normal maintenance procedure. The gear ratio could be varied in four steps from 4:1 on top gear, to 14:1 as the lowest gear. Many GWKs were made before 1914, and were used for touring, competition and even racing.

The French Tweenie appeared in 1913, and was a light four-wheeled car having a 6hp (90mm by 120mm) single-cylinder water-cooled engine and final chain drive from a countershaft, which incorporated friction drive. Settings were provided for seven forward speeds and a reverse.

The successful Violet-Bogey design was produced in 1913 by M. Violet of Paris, who continued to produce cyclecars of original designs for the next decade. The engine and chassis layout was a four-wheeled type with a primary-transmission shaft and a friction disc and secondary-chain drive to a solid rear axle. The 1,088cc (73mm by 130mm) twin-cylinder water-cooled vertical engine was reputed to be capable of developing 22hp at a speed of 2,400rpm, in the special racing form in which it was used in the 1913 Amiens Cyclecar Grand Prix. The inlet over exhaust system was operated by a simple valve gear arrangement with a push-pull rod from a single camshaft, thus avoiding the necessity for external rocker

The Scott Sociable was offered to the British Army during the First World War as a gun carriage. The driver and gunner sat on open mesh steel seating. The passenger and gun could sit facing fore or aft. The gun is a wooden mock-up of a 1908 Light Pattern Vickers machine gun. The War Department did not take up the offer of production. The two-cylinder two-stroke 578cc engine is uncovered, but had a metal cover in use.

Light Car and Cyclecar

Vol. XXII No. 550
Friday June 8, 1923
Registered at the GPO as a Newspaper

Founded 1912
The only Small Car Journal

Mr. A. V. Roe, designer of the world-famous Avro aeroplanes, has built a remarkable single-seater car. A full description appears herein.

The Harper Runabout was made in A.V. Roe's Newton Heath, Manchester, aircraft factory prior to Alliott Verdon Roe's venture into single-seater cars. This is the front page of Light Car and Cyclecar, June 1923, with the cars nestling beneath an Avro Aldershot bomber, Avro's first large plane, of 68ft wing span. The Harper had a considerable amount of non-automobile practice involved in its construction, which leads to the conclusion that Roy Chadwick/A.V. Roe were involved with R.O. Harper in the design of the Harper Runabout. (Peter Harper collection)

arms; this arrangement permitted the use of large valves of 40mm diameter with a high power output. The Grand Prix engine was reported to have been fitted with aluminium-alloy pistons, possibly made by Corbin, which had first appeared in 1910. The single-throw crankshaft was carried on ball bearings. Lubrication was provided by a low-pressure circulating system – a Gobbi carburettor and a Bosch magneto were used.

The Violet-Bogey transmission used a long shaft from the flywheel, which had just sufficient fore and aft movement to allow for declutching, effected by means of a pedal, with a catch to keep the two friction surfaces apart to provide a neutral position. The driving disc was faced with a surface made of compressed paper, across which moved the driven disc which was mounted on a splined cross shaft, in a similar manner to the GWK. The bearing housings of this cross shaft were interconnected with the radius rods securing the rear axle, and had a slight oscillatory movement, so that the pressure between the driving and driven surfaces increased proportionately with the thrust of the rear wheels. The final drive was by chain.

A considerably more complicated friction-driven car was also made in the United States – the water-cooled four-cylinder 3 litre Trumbull, produced by the American Cyclecar Co.

The Carden of 1913 by J.V. Carden was one of the first monocars. The simple shell body, consisting of a wooden framework and metal sheeting, was supported in front on a single coil spring and steering pivot. Steering was effected through a wheel and flexible cables and bobbins. Either a single or twin-cylinder air-cooled JAP engine was mounted in the tail of the, body, immediately behind the driver, which drove the rear axle via a clutch and chains. Its low weight, 3cwt, and a low centre of gravity with minimal frontal area, made it capable of speeds in excess of 80mph, and it was used for track racing as well as other sporting events. In its simplest form it cost under £60, and was later produced in two-seat form. The Dew

The Harper Runabout was advertised as being the 'first cost' of a motorcycle (meaning a motor cycle price) with the ease of control, luxurious springing, absence of balancing support of a car and, in large print: 'THE HARPER RUNABOUT DOES NOT SKID.'

A Tamplin, which still exists, with Mr Wynn Owen.

monocar was a simple open vehicle, with a single-cylinder engine located in front. The drive was by a primary chain to a cross shaft, and the final drive was by two belts. The body provided a single bucket seat, and the steering was of the Ackermann type, controlled by a wheel. A Dew was entered for the Amiens race but had to be modified to a two-seater form as required by the French, by putting a seat behind the driver and behind the rear wheels. This design modification was not a success, however, since the weight redistribution meant that the front wheels had only a nodding acquaintance with the road.

The most elaborate form of cyclecar that appeared before 1914 was the shaft-driven type with two or three-speed gearbox, a live rear axle and a twin-cylinder engine. This type derived more from motor car than motorcycle design and manufacturing technique. In the medium-priced field, namely between £100 and £150, this type was undoubtedly the most practical and popular at this time, since they offered car reliability combined with the convenience, comfort and weather protection of a true car. The designs which appeared had two or three-seat bodies equipped with windscreens, folding cape-cart type hoods, and boots for conveying equipment or luggage. They were capable of speeds up to 40mph, averaging 25mph, and of covering some forty to fifty miles on a gallon of fuel. Established manufacturers of full size motor cars, such as Humber. Swift, Alldays and Onions, Enfield, Douglas, Peugeot, Charron and Adler, endeavoured to produce light cars.

The single-cylinder Humberette, produced by the Humber Co. of Coventry in 1903, was succeeded in 1912 by a new totally updated model, equipped with an 8hp vee-twin cylinder air-cooled engine of 998cc capacity, a leather-lined cone clutch, a three-speed and reverse gearbox attached as a unit to the crankcase, and shaft drive to a rear axle, fitted with a

The 1913 Morris Oxford which must have frightened cyclecar manufacturers with its specification and price.

differential. The differential for most narrow-tracked cyclecars was an expensive luxury and therefore hardly ever fitted. Lubrication was by sight drip-feed as found on motorcycles of that period and for many years after the First World War. Although the car only weighed 7cwt, the two-seat body, with windscreen and hood and tapering bonnet with front gills, gave it the appearance of a scaled-down car. A foot-operated band brake was incorporated behind the gearbox in the transmission shaft and the hand brake operated two external-contracting brakes on drums fitted to the rear wheel hubs. Steering was by rack-and-pinion gearing.

The 1914 model was improved in detail but remained substantially the same in general layout, although a water-cooled version with a front radiator was added. Production ceased in 1915 and the design was not revived after the war. The reasoning probably that the Humberette was not a cheap car to produce, even though it appeared to be a cyclecar. Other examples of the vee-twin, shaft-driven cyclecar included the Chater-Lea, Crouch, Warren-Lambert and Omnium.

The good balance characteristics and even firing periods of the horizontally-opposed form of four-stroke engine recommended itself for use in motorcycles and cars, although comparatively few designers of cars and motorcycles actually adopted it for production, chiefly because it was not an easy unit to install on account of its width. The Douglas cyclecar with the traditional flat twin engine appeared in 1913. One of the earliest cyclecar concerns to adopt this form of engine was the Jowett Co. of Bradford. The Jowett design was originated in 1906. Jowett was one of the very few firms to survive successfully through the development period of the cyclecar, whose basic design of a simple twin-cylinder water-cooled engined car of low weight and economical characteristics, combined with an exceptional capacity for hard work, continued in production over several decades. The Jowett cyclecar was not to finally disappear until the Jowett Bradford van was taken off the market in 1953-1954, when the company failed.

Towards the end of 1912, William Morris, who had a garage in Oxford which had grown out of his cycle shop, unveiled his lightest of light cars at the reasonable price of £175. It was

A Tamplin.

fitted with complete equipment including a British-made four-cylinder White & Poppe and later the American-made 'Continental' engine and had two acetylene head lamps plus two oil-fired side lights, a two-seater 'torpedo' body and a brass 'bull-nose' radiator. This was the Morris Oxford, later to be renamed the Cowley as the Oxford name was used for a larger variant. These cars were destined to have as profound an influence on motoring for the masses in Britain as Henry Ford had exerted in America. The influence of change was complemented by the Austin Seven serving the small car market. These two designs, for a small and medium sized car, were to dominate and force such cars as the Rover 8 and the Bean off the market.

The cyclecar did survive the First World War and for a few years such machines, like the Tamplin and the Blériot Whippet, found a small market with enthusiasts while the Morgan and the GN continued to appeal to the more sporting-minded, who required performance before comfort. Gradually the reduction in the price of small cars, brought about by the advent of quantity production, seduced the family man from his cyclecar devotion.

In 1915 inflation was rampant and the cost of products had risen by a quarter since 1913. The cost of the War was estimated at £3 million per day and the threat of American imports over-running the market was so real that the Chancellor of the Exchequer, Reginald McKenna, imposed a $33\frac{1}{3}\%$ import duty on all cars, but not on commercial vehicles. This had a significant impact on the British automotive industry which was to last for years.

As in America and France there was always an interest in a lightweight car/van built on motorcycle lines and in 1933 the Raleigh Cycle Co., the biggest British bicycle firm, laid down a production line of a three-wheeler two-seater car called the Safety Seven, but within the year abandoned production, as the cost of guarantee work and after sales service of cars was far more onerous than for bicycles. The design was taken on by Tom Williams who left Raleigh and formed Reliant Engineering in Tamworth, north of Birmingham. He produced the Reliant van which, after the Second World War, shed all its motorcycle components to become a three-wheeler, using car technology throughout.

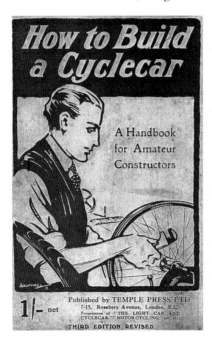

Temple Press in London produced many editions of this handbook.

2
The GN, Racing and
the Development of the GN

Archie Nash and Ron Godfrey first met in 1905 when they signed on as first-year students for the City and Guilds course at Finsbury, North London, in Mechanical Engineering. Archibald Goodman Frazer Nash was born in India in 1889, and had served two brief stints at sea and worked at the Post Office telephone factory at Holloway. Ron Godfrey was born in 1887 near London, and his first sight of motoring was the 1896 Emancipation Run from London to Brighton. In 1901 Godfrey's father gave his son a present, which was to influence the GN concept considerably, for he gave him a Clement. This engine was also known in Britain as the Clement-Garrard. Godfrey fitted it to his bicycle. 'It was a beautifully made little engine with which I travelled many miles,' he said.

Godfrey started his career at five shillings a week as a junior clerk for Werner Motors, the concessionaires for Werner Frères of Paris. The Werner brothers were of Russian, rather than German descent. The Werner motorcycle was one of the great makes in the beginnings of the motorcycle industry. Godfrey ran messages. He left Werners in 1904, for they had fallen behind in design and then the firm panicked and re-designed the whole machine incorporating every fault and vice possible.

Nash and Godfrey in the 1904 period separately built, but did not complete, various types of 'car'; Godfrey endeavoured to build a steam cyclecar using a Locomobile two-cylinder engine. In 1905 he sold Nash his Clement motorcycle engine and Nash fitted it into the

The first GN Quad with a JAP engine in the grounds of The Elms, Hendon (Archie's mother's house).

The 1913 GN. There was no reverse and only two forward speeds. It was a simple modification to give the car three speeds and reverse or, for a competition car like Kim and Bluebottle, four forward speeds.

frame of a Star pedal-cycle and also into the frame of his first 'creep-about', which he used in the grounds of The Elms – his mother's home in Hendon. Nash's mother was one of the first women doctors to qualify and practise in India, from where she had returned after the death of her husband.

After a short time with Renault working 'free', meaning that he was not paid, Nash joined Godfrey at Willans & Robinson (later to become English Electric, GEC & Alsthom), of Rugby, to serve a two-year apprenticeship, and they shared lodgings with M.V. Roberts at 1 York Street, Rugby. Archie Nash is listed as Fraser Nash in his enrolment document; this may have been to differentiate him from another Nash – but the fact it was mis-spelt with 'S' instead of 'Z' probably indicates that some zealous clerk at a much later date had interpolated this. They hired a large barn in Rugby for five shillings a week in which they installed a gas engine that was coupled up to a hired lathe. The problem was to control the speed of the engine when the lathe was running free, as the gas engine had only two speeds: stop and go. This was solved by buying from Willans & Robinson's scrap heap a large emery wheel at the going scrap rate of 2s 6d per hundredweight. When the engine was running free a large drill was pressed up against the grinding wheel by anyone who would care to volunteer for this operation. Further experimental work was carried out on cyclecar construction and Frazer Nash started to build his second 'creep-about'; this was never finished and Godfrey built a three-wheeled 'cycle-car' with a wooden frame and an Antoine engine.

In 1909 Nash left the company, as the works were on part-time, while Godfrey stayed for the remaining six months of the apprenticeship. Nash had to take convalescence after an industrial accident and in this time he built his first motor car to go properly, under its own power. This car, another 'creepabout', used a Peugeot vee-twin motorcycle engine which Dr Nash found herself unwittingly owning as she had acted as guarantor for her son in this purchase. The car was fitted with two-speed chain transmission, but on the first run on public roads the fact was demonstrated that engine braking was not enough.

While still convalescing Nash made a trip to Scarborough accompanied by his brother, Malcolm. The trip was bedevilled with engineering failure; they pushed the car for the last

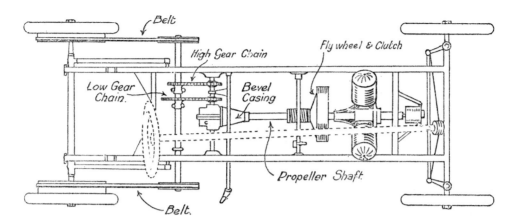

The chassis of a 1913 GN.

seven miles. The main lesson learnt was that of how to deal with vibration. On Nash's return home he went into partnership with J. Robertson Brown, and the intention was to call the partnership 'Nash & Brown'. Archie Nash built a cyclecar chassis and Brown had a body fitted and this car was seen by E.M.P. Boileau, editor of *The Motor Cycle*, who wrote the car up at length in *The Motor Cycle* of 10 November 1910, entitling the article 'A Sociable Quadricycle'. Nash saw this article, in which no mention was made of him or the partnership, and immediately got in touch with *The Motor Cycle*. Boileau agreed that rather than have any trouble, it would be much better to write another article to put the matter right. As soon as Godfrey had finished his apprenticeship at Rugby he returned home to Hendon, and on his way he called in to see Nash at The Elms. He was told of *The Motor Cycle* article and the pair of them immediately fell to and started to build the car that was to become the first GN.

That is to say they designed it on the Friday to manufacture on the Monday. Boileau then wrote up the GN Quad, standing for Quadricar, in *The Motor Cycle* of 28 December 1910. When he visited them prior to writing the article, they had stuck up on the walls of Mrs Nash's barn, part of the out-buildings of The Elms, the drawings they had made on the City and Guilds course, as Archie Frazer-Nash said many years later 'to lend an air of verisimilitude'. The article said:

> There have been a number of attempts in the past to produce a passenger vehicle which is little more expensive in initial cost and running than the popular motor bicycle. To attain these ends, lightness is a sine qua non, but lightness and strength do not go hand in hand, and most of the early attempts to satisfy popular requirements lacked rigidity. On November 10th last we illustrated a new form of sociable quadcar on which we had been allowed a trial, and that machine has been spoken of very favourably. On this page we illustrate the latest form of a GN runabout, of which the quadcar previously referred to was the forerunner. It must be admitted at once that the design is very striking, the bodywork being particularly neat. A point to recommend it is that it is no experiment or suggested design, but the outcome of two years' experience with this type of vehicle. It is made in three different models, the price varying

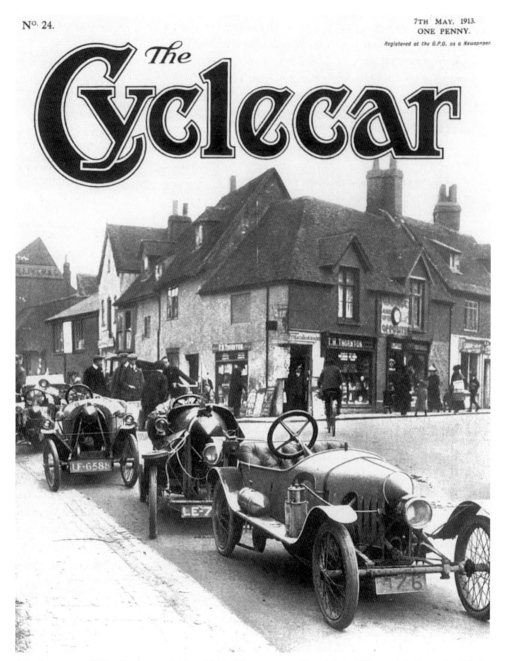

The front cover of The Cyclecar, *7 May 1913. The prototype Grand Prix GN posed in front of a Sabella and a 1912 GN. That issue announced that the Amiens race for Cyclecars had attracted thirty-one entries.*

according to equipment, but the same outline is common to all. Firstly, it is compact and as narrow as possible to reduce wind resistance. The 8h.p. engine, which is of the V-type, twin-cylinder, air-cooled variety, is situated in front, the cooling being assisted by means of a fan. A refinement worthy of mention is that the carburettor is fitted with a pilot jet for slow running. The petrol tank is torpedo-shaped, and placed above the engine. Its capacity is sufficient for 200 miles. The frame is suspended on large tubular axles by cantilever plate springs duplicated in front. Steering is by twin wire rope, acting without jockeys or guides, and turning the wheels only as in standard car practice. The two-speed gear is placed amidships, the drive being communicated from the engine by means of a chain. The final drive may be by chain or V-belt depending upon the model selected. The gear gives a direct drive on both speeds. Radius rods are used to control the movement of the rear axle. Push pedals operate clutch and brake, and an extra hand brake is also fitted.

In the case of the de luxe model internal expanding brakes are used, but on the 'sporting' models, belt-rim brakes. The tyres are heavy voiturette 650 by 65mm section. The weights are given by the makers as follows: Sporting single-seater, 230lb; 7ft wheelbase. Sporting two-seater, 300lb; 7ft 9ins wheel-base. De luxe two-seater, 400lb; 7ft 9ins wheel-base. It should be observed that the two-seater runabouts have side-by-side seats, rendering conversation an easy matter. All parts, excepting the engines J.A.P. or Peugeot, magnetos Bosch, and minor fittings, are made at the works of Godfrey and Nash, Elms Motor Works, Golders' Green Road, Hendon.

The response from this second article was sufficient to show that there was a demand – they did not have to advertise, all they had to do was to produce the cars. Raymond Morgan produced almost overnight a catalogue in which were listed the 'standard' and 'de luxe' chassis; a strong recommendation was made in the accompanying letter to the 'de luxe' chassis as it incorporated all the lessons learnt in the manufacture of the prototypes. Morgan, whose nickname was 'Chisel', also drew the sketches of the models, and the slogan was coined, 'The comfort of a car with the speed of a motor-cycle!' The 8hp JAP engine was fitted as being the logical power unit available. This brochure naturally provided an overview of the types of motor vehicle available with the damning remark about sidecar outfits: 'Speed can only be attempted…on dead straight roads.'

Three orders with one-third deposits were received, and six weeks delivery promised, practically by return of post, and a further four or five arrived in the next few weeks. Godfrey and Nash pooled their resources and the first works were established in the outhouses behind Archie's mother's house, with two foot treadle lathes, a drilling machine and an assorted collection of hand tools. Ron Godfrey said in a report in *The Light Car* of 1933, on the occasion of that magazine dropping 'and Cycle-Car' from its title:

The first order was completed after many months and numerous promises for delivery had been broken. It is a Saturday and our customer, who so far we have only known by name, arrives stating that he wishes to drive away at once as he has a 220-mile journey. Archie Nash greets him but I, hovering for a furtive last-minute adjustment, notice that he is not quite his serene self. Perhaps he is thinking our masterpiece does not look quite so sleek as the catalogue illustrations… How cheering it was in 1911 to read in a letter appearing in Motor Cycling, *written by our first customer that the engine, the wheels and bits of wood had 'vindicated the possibilities of the cycle-car' and were 'the owner's magic carpet'.*

That first owner was George W. Walmsley of Cleator Moor, Cumberland. He wrote a three-page article in *Motor Cycling* in November 1911 which told of the journeys he had made and the difficulties he had had with belt drives, ignition and brakes in the first 300 miles of ownership, but the whole article was warm with praise and he concluded:

> *As to reliability, I do not see what there is to go wrong, beyond what can be easily adjusted on the road by the average motorcyclist. The engine is an 8hp JAP, and if one cannot keep that power plant in tune, the deficiency will be personal. The carburettor is the standard 1911 motorcycle B and B, and the ignition is by Bosch magneto, with coil and accumulator for starting the front cylinder. The gears are very simple, and of the sliding dog type. The large double disc clutch, operated by pedal, is simplicity itself. The GN has evidently passed through a long period of eliminations, and evolved into a production like the drawings of a master cartoonist, whose few lines seem so simple, yet mean so much, and bespeak the more prescience and study in the primary stages.*
>
> *I can make the usual disclaimer in a more original way, as my only personal acquaintance with Messrs Godfrey and Nash was when I went to Hendon after many postponements, hoping to drive the GN home to Cumberland, but I am afraid it was only hard words I used in my disappointment. I believe, since, that my wait was profitable. I am sure I have a far, far better car for waiting.*

Cleator is a small village and it was hoped the G.W. Walmsley or his family could be located, but this was not to be. His place of business was located, but the Walmsleys had long since gone.

The first few cars were hardly delivered before the drawbacks of the original design were apparent. The fifty-degree vee-twin JAP motorcycle engines had very little balance, poor low-speed torque and no flywheel worthy of the name. The motorcycle engine was obviously hopeless for the job of driving a car. Most motorcycle engines of the day were incapable of idling, and vibrated badly. Further, the small flywheels and crude carburettors of the period together with the inferior balance of a narrow vee-engine, caused driving in traffic to be very tricky for fear of stopping the engine. One of the main troubles was that the very long initial primary chain drive tended to pull the flywheels apart. Ron Godfrey was interviewed by Sam Clutton for an article which appeared in *Motor Sport* on the occasion of that magazine's thirtieth birthday:

> *Starting was on the wire-and-ratchet principle with a return spring, and this worked well enough except when the engine back-fired and wound the operator back into the imitation radiator. Again, owing to the carburation defects, re-starting was difficult, and when driving in traffic, owners generally idled at high revs, which shook off wings in a few hundred miles and overheated the engine. To overcome this, fans were fitted, but not infrequently the blades came off and stabbed the petrol tank. As the petrol then poured on to a hot engine a cheerful blaze usually resulted.*

It was almost an item of creed that everything that could not be cast should be made in the round, as the partners did not have a milling machine. The original dog clutches were made in the round with two pegs per clutch, consequently the first cars were fitted with peg clutches for the gear selection. The traditional GN and the later GN and Frazer Nash dog clutch had to wait till they could afford to purchase a 'miller'. These original cars had final chain transmission by side chains on each side of the car, giving different ratios, so that only one rear wheel was driven at a time. All these early cars were either re-bought by the firm or were returned when it was obvious that some redesign had got to be carried out. Godfrey used his Antoine engine and they built the prototype of the next model, which was sold to C.S. Burney. The first six de luxe chassis and the Burney car were all produced in the stables and it was obvious that more space was needed. They moved the manufacturing to 'The Burroughs' in Hendon – a series of sheds in which other small businesses existed, mostly by the skin of their teeth. The new model used the same vee-twin 8hp JAP engine, but the primary chain drive was now by an equally long belt. This prevented snatching but substituted belt-slip since there was always a certain amount of oil outside the JAP engine of those days. Two chains gave the speeds selected by peg clutch to the countershaft, which then drove both rear wheels by belts mounted on the outside of the chassis. The original design had springs above and below the front axle and Waverley threatened litigation as this was their design; the bottom spring was replaced with a radius arm and this gave superior steering and road-holding. It was at this stage that Cecil Whitehead, known as 'Snowy', offered to put up £1,000 as capital to get the firm on to a more business-like footing. He was the owner of a GN, liked it and thought the car had a future. A company was registered called GN Ltd, instead of the previous loosely named Godfrey & Nash, which had never been registered, and the official company address was The Elms Works, Burroughs, Hendon.

The tools at Nash's home had all been foot or hand-powered, but at the Burroughs they fitted up the Clement engine to provide limited belt-driven power. Godfrey also bought an ancient Lenoir gas engine, from the beginnings of the French industrial revolution, which worked on a strange two-cycle principle, where the firing stroke was the last half of the down stroke. In this condition it hardly developed any power at all so Godfrey converted it to a more modern heat-cycle principle. The reinforced ash chassis was used in all GNs made before the First World War – production stopped in 1915. The main difference between GN and the other numerous cyclecar manufacturers was the engine. The majority of cyclecar manufacturers in Britain and the rest of the world had one thing in common – they all used proprietary parts when they were available, and that meant, nine times out of ten in Britain, the JAP engine.

The engine that Godfrey designed was based on that same Clement engine that he had sold to Nash years before. This engine had an overhung crank and was ideally suited to be made with lathes and the products of a foundry. Overhung crankshafts mean a long bearing on one side of the engine and no main bearing at the other side, though there may be valve and ignition take offs. Godfrey scaled up the single-cylinder Clement engine and made a ninety-degree vee-twin with an outside flywheel. As well as using the JAP engine, experiments had been carried out using a Peugeot 8hp vee-twin engine which suffered from similar drawbacks as the JAP, but the Peugeot cylinder barrels were borrowed for the new GN design and the first dozen or so of the new engines were fitted with certain parts bought from Messrs Peugeot. These barrels were fitted with non-detachable heads and an automatic inlet valve. The prototype GN engine was fitted with this automatic inlet valve but subsequently they applied a push rod and rocker to the Peugeot head, which was far more fashionable! During 1911 and early 1912 these Peugeot parts, cylinder barrel with a non-detachable head, valves and pistons, were fitted to all the GNs. When asked if Peugeot knew or minded, Godfrey said, 'We never asked.'

The car to be fitted with the prototype of this engine was built in time for the Hendon Air Show in 1911, not for exhibition or use there, but the occasion was imprinted in Nash's mind by the fact that it would not start, and when they pushed it, it ran away and the steering wheel had to be tweaked to turn the car into a wall to stop it savaging the returning throngs from the air show.

Osmond Hill, one of the early owners and the joint secretary of the newly formed Cycle-Car Club, suggested that bonnet sides, hung from the cylindrical petrol tank, would improve the looks of the car. In 1911-1912 the word 'cyclecar' replaced the previous duocar, quadri-cycle or quadcar, as the generally accepted name for describing such cars.

This new car was the first successful GN model, and with the heavy flywheel it meant that the cyclic variations of the engine were better damped; and consequently the primary drive reverted to chain. Though the engine's tick-over was not good, it was a sensational improve-ment on the JAP. Previously the engine had been parallel to the frame, but in 1912 it was placed across the frame. GN heads and barrels were fitted, and the two exhaust ports faced forward, sticking out of the sides of the bonnet.

The new cylinder heads gave a very low compression ratio and so a lump of metal was cast in, over the piston in the head, to improve it. This gave a marked increase in horse-power. Frazer Nash and Godfrey thought this fearfully 'un-engineering', and it was not until 1921 that they finally got around to producing a much cleaner cylinder-head design, with the same compression ratio, and there was a definite drop in power. They had discovered the

An ultra long wheel base 1914 GN with belt final drive and three seats. Ron Godfrey said that the Russian Count who had paid for it, never came to collect and after the war they reduced the chassis length and rebodied the car as a conventional two seater and this may well be the 1913 car that still survives.

squish Ricardo head principle years before Ricardo. Another man to make the same discovery was C.B. Franklin, who had modified his Indian motorcycle engine the same way; O.C. Godfrey, Ron Godfrey's cousin, who had won the 1911 TT on an Indian, eventually managed to see Franklin's cylinder-heads and came and told Godfrey about it. Godfrey and Nash did not realise at that time that they had fortuitously done the same thing.

The engine being placed across the chassis helped the cooling and made sustained high-speed running possible. Touring cars of the pre-war time were limited in power and road holding and were rarely capable of achieving 45mph. This can hardly be regarded as high speed, though it undoubtedly was seen so by the magistrates of the time.

This new GN engine had its cylinder heads as separate castings and the barrels and heads were held down with a pair of yokes tensioned by two long studs into the crankcase. This obviously posed problems in tightening down, due to differential expansion of the various parts. It was not unknown for the studs to be over-tightened and, when the engine got really hot, for a piece of cylinder head to detach itself. Many an innocent bystander had his fingers burnt when trying to pick up the pieces off the road to give them back to the intrepid motorist.

The works racing/sports cars were capable of up to 60mph and the first GN entry for a race meeting was at Brooklands in 1912. The first cyclecar race to be held at Brooklands was in 1913 on handicap, and Nash and Whitehead finished first and second. Nash was driving the 'Streamer' (streamlined by GN standards), and averaged just over 42mph, with a fastest lap of 54mph, under squally conditions.

Archie Nash and Ron Godfrey were together in the 'office' of the Elms Motor Works, which had been the office for the Chinese Laundry that had lately vacated the premises. They were discussing the recurring theme of each issue of the January 1913 *Cyclecar* magazine. The theme was that it was certain that a Cyclecar Grand Prix would take place over the same course as the French Grand Prix, probably on Sunday 13 July. Archie Nash was eulogising at length over the undoubted fun there would be in entering a continental motor race and, almost in parentheses, that there would be positive advantages for the firm of a good performance by GNs in such a race. Ron Godfrey, in his quiet way, pointed out that 'a good result was unlikely since it was difficult enough to go to London and back without having an involuntary stop.' Hendon to London was one thing, at five to seven miles, but a Grand Prix, even for cyclecars, was 250 or more racing miles, the pertinence of Ron Godfrey's doubts was undeniable. The 1912 GN was by no means everything that a car should be – over simple, almost crude in parts, with a lower engineering content than either of the principal partners had intended when they launched the car on the market in early 1911. Almost without discussion they knew they would enter for the Grand Prix and the whole car had to be redesigned there and then, from stem to stern; reliability had to be built in and, as Ron Godfrey said, 'some of the woodscrews replaced by nuts and bolts'. Ron Godfrey, in later years, said that in January of 1913 they were introducing changes, but that month changed their lives. 'If we had not decided to enter for the 1913 Amiens Cyclecar Grand Prix, there would have been no post-war GN model ready for manufacture, no Frazer Nash and certainly no HRG.'

The 1913 Amiens Grand Prix staged, as an *hors d'oeuvre* on the previous day, the Cycle-car Grand Prix. Nash's crankpin came loose in the race (one of the few times this happened), and Whitehead split one of his cylinder heads, due to over-enthusiastic tightening up of all the bolts just before the start.

The new GN, known as the GP model, had gone a long way towards the post-war drive specification. The drive was taken from the flywheel by the GN plate clutch, via a propshaft to the bevel box, thence via two chains for the two speeds (still no reverse) to a countershaft, which drove the back axle by belts. The three-speed and reverse transmission came in 1914, still using belt final drive.

In the spring of 1914 the works were again moved, this time to a brand new factory of 10,000-12,000sq.ft capacity called the Etna Works, in Albert Road, Hendon. Whitehead had by this time sold out his shares to Lt Wilkinson, and newer machine tools were bought. The rate of production of cars built up during 1914, so that two cars a week were being made. The GN cyclecar of 1914 cost £107 complete; in small print in the catalogue it said that accessories included a windscreen, hood, spare wheel with tyre, set of lamps, horn, pump and tools which totalled £16 3s. Instead of the standard two-speed transmission it was possible to have an extra speed for another £3.

C.W. Cook wrote in *The Autocar* on 29 March 1940 of his GN reminiscences, and the following is an extract from the article, covering the 1914-1915 period:

> On one car, a long wheelbase three-seater with a dickey in the tail, the owner discovered that the entire flooring of the third seat had dropped out, seriously inconveniencing the owner's mother-in-law. And the owner was overheated too – he waved aside a suggestion that the whole affair had been carefully planned (regardless of expense) to relieve rheumatic tendencies on the part of the old lady, and was only appeased by an offer to redesign the model by replacing sundry nails by woodscrews. The makers, always advocates of the gay life, thoughtfully positioned the magneto immediately below the carburettor, which, needing vigorous flooding before starting up from cold, doused the slip ring and contact breaker with highly volatile spirit. On cranking the engine, it was best first to turn off the petrol, then to smother the fire with an old cap. Experienced owners were able to judge to a nicety when to turn on the petrol again. Too short a wait meant another flare-up, while delay caused the disappearance of what was undeniably the first unpremeditated 'easy-start' hot spot.

Incidentally, the beautifully curved induction pipe was another triumph of adaptation – cycle-trade factors were undoubtedly surprised by the large and consistent orders for sets of push-bike handlebars, which were used to carry the mixture to the cylinders 'of thermally efficient size'. The magnetos, also, never started life as suppliers of sparks for 90-degree twins. They were originally 60-degree or 55-degree, 'Converted by Special Process in our Own Works'. This resulted in certain difficulties with regard to field position and spark intensity, but a successful compromise was arrived at by allotting maximum spark to one cylinder, which was officially known as the 'starting cylinder', and the engine was 'revved' until the other cylinder chimed in. Gear ratios were usually determined, due to the variety of transmissions used in the pre-1914 period, not by calculation, but by chalking flywheel rim and tyre and counting relative revolutions while the chassis was slowly pushed along a level floor. It was possible, by unskilled or over-hasty manipulation, to engage second gear before first had entirely freed; the resulting catastrophe was known as 'two gears at once', which, bending the bevel shaft, imparted an entirely novel motion to the bevel box and its contents and caused a pumping motion of the clutch pedal. This persisted until another 'two gears' was effected when, by the law of averages, the bevel shaft usually became straight again. The brakes acted upon the belt rims and were very effective forwards, but almost

The GN factory. Later to be taken over by Clayton Mineral Waters, who removed the GN pediments fixed to the roof.

entirely useless in the backward direction. 'This peculiarity came to my notice', wrote C.W. Cook, 'when I ran out of petrol half-way up Netherhall Gardens.' The works in which cycle-cars were made lacked the rigid discipline and the impersonal relationships of modern factories. At one time GN's main shop was divided off into various departments by barriers of wire netting, which, in certain parts, were almost invisible at night. The GN was started by a detachable handle positioned on the off-side of the car and so dimensioned that undue enthusiasm on the part of the 'swinger' brought the knuckles of the right hand into violent contact with the road surface.

The 1915 catalogue was full of gems (read by today's standards). In 1915 the GN was unassailable in value for money and performance, so the opening paragraphs, written by Raymond Morgan, GN's official PR man (years before many firms had a spokesperson), were entitled to be headed '*Simplicity, a science and a virtue*'. In the section on the transmission, reference was made to their competitors with their '*ordinary car gear-box*' and a suggestion made that '*a momentary carelessness in its operation may mean a possible twenty pounds worth of damage, INVOLVING TEDIOUS DISMOUNTING and re-erecting of inaccessible parts.*' Much was made of the 'vibrationless' GN engine and the cylinders of 'thermally efficient size'.

The 1915 Grand Prix GN was available with four-speed forward transmission or three-speed and reverse, still with the final belt drive. Renold chain of $\frac{5}{8}$in pitch was the standard fitment for all pre-war GNs using chain-drive. After the war they changed to $\frac{3}{4}$in pitch, which size was later used in the Frazer Nash. Money was being made and it was decided to enter for the Dangerfield Trophy, to be held in the Isle of Man in September 1914 as well as for the 1914 running of the Cyclecar Grand Prix in Amiens. They were developing the push rod ohv engine, later to be known as the Kim engine.

An officer having put on his wartime uniform for the christening of his child in 1925. The vicar is behind the wheel of a 1913 GP GN. The GN, having been pulled out of a shed for the photograph, is fitted with acetylene lighting and wire and bobbin steering. The front hub phosphor bronze bushes of this pensioned-off cyclecar are worn out giving negative camber.

Sheret, an inspired blacksmith of a man, had been responsible for the rortier cams fitted in 1913, but the engines were not up to really serious development. The bottom end was quite sound, so an engine was designed, that was to become known as the Kim engine. The capacity was still 1,100cc, given by twin cylinders with the standard bore and stroke of 84mm by 98mm, but more generously finned than the standard barrels. The cylinder heads were made of bronze with the pair of 47mm diameter valves at a wide angle in almost hemispherical combustion chambers. The valve operation was by pushrods and rockers, which were forked to pick up the valve stems halfway down their length. The idea for this was 'borrowed' from the Prince Henry 27/80 Austrian-Daimler (Godfrey at the time owned one of these successful sports racer cars). A very narrow, staggered, two-seater body was fitted to Kim, but as an alternative, there was a single-seater body in which guise the car competed in sprints in 1914, driven by Nash, when it was more or less unbeatable. The outbreak of war caused the cancellation of the Dangerfield Trophy, and racing cars were put on one side.

The beginning of the war was 'business as usual', and the works announced the 1915 range, which was the same as 1914, but with the addition of the 'Touring' model; this was the low price cyclecar. The Touring was a two-speeder with a very light body, no complications whatsoever, and with practically everything as an extra, added onto the basic price of eighty-eight guineas.

During 1915, the car side of GNs came slowly to a halt and war work was substituted. The works made hundreds of thousands of detonator containers for HE shells, and also one order for 100 gun-stands, which were to enable aeroplane pilots to fire a machine-gun through a revolving propeller. The stands consisted of an ash frame on which was mounted a Vickers machine-gun, a GN engine and an armoured propeller.

Archie Nash joined up under the Lord Hugh Cecil scheme of 1915 as a technical officer, for he had worked for the War Office earlier that year. He was finally commissioned in 1918 and was flying before the war was over. One of the problems of the war, which was ultimately solved by Constantinesco, was the feed of bullets through a propeller's blades without actually hitting them. Nash decided that a phased hydraulic pulse was the answer, but the changes in temperature of an aeroplane at altitude affected the operation and the War Office settled for the Constantinesco hydraulic scheme.

In 1916, Sheret built himself a novel GN at the works in his spare time. He fitted the engine behind the driving compartment, and fitted it in line with the chassis whence it was connected to a cross-shaft by means of a chain – this shaft carried the normal three-speed and reverse chain-drive to the next shaft which was the back axle. A replica of this car was also made by another employee of the time, E. Fresher. Sheret proved that the final belts were unnecessary, so only a small modification was required from the 1915 range to make the GN ready for the post-war era by 1916. The fuel tank had been moved into the scuttle in 1915 and the familiar V-pointed dummy radiator shell was produced, fitted with expanded wire mesh, so that the uninitiated would think the radiator was radiating. The engine was modified in two ways for the post-war market. Four holding-down studs were used to hold each head and cylinder to the crank-case, and the timing chest was reduced in depth. This got over the problem of fractured cylinder heads, and the smaller timing chest reduced the valve noise considerably; prior to this there was no need for the GN to have a horn, as the engine noises would give adequate warning of the car's approach. The ash frame which had been the standard wear was dropped, not because it had been unsatisfactory – in fact it had been completely successful – but because a steel channel section was regarded as being more

L.A. Cushman at the wheel of Bluebottle. Ron Godfrey campaigned the 1913 Bluebottle through to 1921. The specification was a pre-war ash chassis with a Kim engine. After the war the car was fitted with an up-to-date 'radiator' shell.

likely to impress purchasers. The wire and bobbin steering was also dropped and a conventional steering-box with a drop-arm arrangement substituted. The wire and bobbin was direct, simple, and when it needed attention, the cables fraying gave an owner several thousand miles of warning before they became dangerous.

The wire and bobbin steering gave Godfrey and Nash much pleasure. If they did not like a customer they would re-wrap the wire round the bobbin in the opposite direction, this meant that the steering wheel worked the opposite way. As the customer departed the principals of GN Ltd would rush to the door and apply their eyes to spy-holes to watch the almost immediate accident, usually at very low speeds. A.C. Armstrong, the first editor of *The Cycle-Car*, who was regarded as a friend of the partners, had to submit to this operation being carried out on his GN on one of his frequent visits to the Etna Works.

With the war over, it became obvious that the Etna Works was ridiculously small for the orders that were pouring in by January 1919. Having dispensed with belt final drive, the GN was a modern-looking car that was cheap to buy. The post-war prototype included no modification to make the car run better, but the modifications added up to making the GN a modern design. The engines were generally run for ten minutes in the erection shop and then were fitted into a chassis; this chassis then underwent a one-day test. There was then an extended test with an unpainted body and then a final test after the cars were finished.

An agreement was negotiated with the British Gregoire Agency Co., who had a large works at East Hill, Wandsworth. An exchange of capital took place and GNs received a cheque of £70,000 for their valuation from Gregoire's. The valuable start that GN enjoyed with their post-war model being ready was lost with the change of plans caused by the new factory. By March 1919, Morgans were producing their three-wheeler as fast as they could, and were probably making twenty cars a week whilst all that could be claimed by GN Ltd was that two models were in the course of preparation, though the works at Hendon were still in production and producing two or three cars a week.

The Cycle-Car Club had been dominated by the GN before the war; A.C. Armstrong, Editor of the *The Light Car and Cycle-Car*, and Osmond Hill were both committee members, with Frank Thomas as Secretary, and all were GN owners. Nash was also a committee member. After the war the club changed its name to the Junior Car Club, usually known as the JCC, and a social meeting was held in April 1919. More Morris Cowleys were present than any other make of car; the cyclecar appeared already to have become *démodé*, and so it became incumbent on the cyclecar manufacturers to produce more attractive and sophisticated cars. The Buckingham, and the AV Monocar hardly raised cyclecar standards and the Morgan was already regarded as a superior, more sporting form of the motorcycle and sidecar. In the world of car design of the twenty-first century, the monocoque form of construction is regarded as one of the significant design/manufacturing changes of the 1930s which was taken up by all types of motor car manufacturers by the 1950s, including Grand Prix single-seaters. The Carden could not be regarded as a world leader, but Carden's use of a box construction with the flat upper wing on each side was well before its time.

The Autocar of June 1920 commented:

> It is rather disappointing to notice that the post-war cycle-car is still very far from being accepted
> as a utility vehicle. Hundreds are being sold. So far as I am able to gauge the market, they are
> mostly being bought by motor-cyclists of the semi-sporting type – an audacious and much-
> enduring type of motorist, who is usually rather reckless financially and technically much more
> efficient than the average car owner.

In 1919 anything could be sold, and even derelict ex-WD cars fetched many hundreds of pounds in auction sales.

The Olympia Motor Show, held in late 1919 to display the 1920 models, had on the GN stand a highly-polished GN Vitesse chassis, with the ioe valve engine, and a Standard two-seater car complete at £184. The Vitesse GN weighed 8cwt with fuel and oil, and was 100lb lighter in weight than the Standard two-seater. *The Autocar* gave the GN an excellent write-up in December 1919: 'Growing as it did from a belt-driven, half motorcycle, half car, built somewhat obscurely in a shed at Hendon by enthusiasts.'

The Autocar was somewhat perturbed by the oiling system used by GNs – the oil tank on the running-board bearing a hand-plunger pump which forced oil to the crankshaft end bearing, and thence to the timing gear and cylinders. *The Autocar* explained rather heavily that this simple type of lubrication works perfectly on heavily laden motorcycle side-car outfits.

Production at East Hill started in late 1919, and by the end of 1920, over 500 people were being employed and a maximum rate of fifty-eight cars in a week was established, with a record month of 220 cars. This was big business, and a night-shift had to be introduced. The factory was well organised, with works managers, service and sales managers and heads of various departments – machine shop, experimental, and racing. Ron Godfrey was an ideal person for running such an establishment.

GNs found themselves emerging from the chaos of tooling up for mass production in 1920, as part of their endeavour to become a major motor car manufacturer and the aim was to satisfy their agents. The agents wanted cars to sell, they also wanted a first class back-up service of spare parts, manuals, advertising and promotional matter. H.R. Morgan was a tower of strength in making sure that the promotional material was available and he also recommended the absolute necessity of a decent spare parts manual. H.R. Morgan used his christian name, Raymond, professionally so 'Raymond Publicity' was marked on advertising material produced for GN.

Several attempts were made to produce a parts list and, in the end, Godfrey accepted Morgan's suggestion that they should take a car off the production line, put it in a shed, take it apart, photograph the parts, and give each part a number. This was done and the manual was a great success, there could be no doubt that a manufacturer who produced such a manual was in the business to stay. Service engineers of the calibre of Capt. Easte, who toured the country, materially increased the firm's standing. There were also produced official spare parts price lists and again in this, it is possible to detect the hand of H.R. Morgan. Godfrey thought the percentage price uplift made to the standard costings rather steep, but Nash chuckled with glee at the sheer nerve of it, though by no means were the prices out of line with other manufacturers.

The sequel to the story of the production of the spare parts manual was that in 1922 there was a form of stock taking and the car that had been taken apart had been painstakingly taken out of the works by an entrepreneurial workman, part by part, and presumably reassembled! The catalogues were all well-produced, but the instruction books were thin by the standards of the day, though the 1920 and subsequent issues did incorporate a paragraph saying:

> *If this instructional booklet seems to contain fewer pages than might have been expected, it is only necessary to remember the number of pages which would normally be included under 'Cooling System', but which in the case of the GN, with its perfect air cooling, are superfluous, together with the safeguards often issued by manufacturers in the defence of 'fragile design'.*

Students of motoring history will be well aware of the subtle and free form of advertising practised by S.F. Edge, in the motoring journals of the day, in advertising the merits of the Napier and AC Cars by writing many letters. GN Ltd were also constant letter writers under many headings, notably those of cyclecars, transmissions and especially air cooling. Much was made of the observed RAC run made by R.C. Mundy, from London to Edinburgh, in his GN, without once stopping the engine. A letter to *The Autocar* in 1920, signed by GN Ltd, said:

> *In 1912 an 8hp gas engine which formed part of the power unit for driving the workshop plant broke down. We immediately installed one of our air-cooled engines. This engine carried on the whole work of the gas engine for six days, after which period the latter came into operation again. During the time the air-cooled engine was functioning, no auxiliary cooling was used or found necessary, while the daily running of the engine was nine hours continuous, except for a one-hour break at mid-day.*

Later in the letter reference was made to Mundy's run: 'Once the engine had been started in London, it was not stopped till the car arrived in Edinburgh, and during the time that the driver and RAC official were having meals, the engine was still running.'

The 1921 winner of the 1,100cc class of the 200-Mile Race. Archie Nash has L.A. Cushman in the passenger seat who was the senior development mechanic at GN. Cushman later became a senior director at the Fairmile in the production of the Invicta, Railton and the Fairmile MTBs and MGBs.

The main difficulty faced by GNs before the 1920-1921 recession was that there were very few capable garage mechanics, and those with any pretensions to skill eschewed the humble cyclecar, so that in many cases the owners had to do their own maintenance. Most of the owners were first owners, and the standards of maintenance were appallingly low. Charles Lewington became the service manager in 1920, and he wrote of those early days in a *Chain Gang Gazette* of 1963 in which he said:

The amount of work was really formidable, as there were then quite a number of GNs on the road in the hands of very ignorant and un-mechanical owners, and the sorts of troubles that they ran into, largely through ignorance and mis-handling, were extraordinary. Quite apart from the dozens of letters daily, which kept two typists going hard at it from opening to closing hours, it was decided to start two travelling service representatives. This, I think, was the first, or if not the first then certainly the second, arrangement of its kind, the idea being to system-atically call on all owners to carry out minor adjustments, free of charge, but to make a charge of so much per hour for any major work such as decarbonisation, etc. This scheme was highly successful, as witness the enormous volume of correspondence congratulating GNs on the idea and the two travelling representatives on their courtesy and efficiency. Even the most dissatis-fied owners became converts after a visit from one of these two travelling ambassadors.

*　　The travelling representatives – whose duty was, of course, to report to me on their return with a detailed list of what had been done, from which I could decide on what charges were to be made to each owner on whom they had called - were obviously very efficient and even more*

In 1919 the ohv Vitesse engine came into being which was the standard crankcase with a new barrel and cylinder head.

important was their keenness on the job and the fun which they derived from it. They were Captain Easte and Duffield, whose brother was editor of that long defunct but excellent magazine Auto. Large numbers of cars were going out and daily being called for by all sorts and conditions of persons, many of whom appeared rather surprising people to own so stark and noisy a vehicle. However, they all seemed enthusiastic, and those who possessed even the rudiments of motor knowledge had great fun and very good service from the old type GN. Needless to say, there were others who really never stood a chance. Their ignorance was really devastating. One farmer of my acquaintance complained that the 'fat' was coming out of his bevel-box.

On being asked to amend this term to 'grease', he contradicted me flatly and said 'No, this was good pork dripping!' The positioning of the works at East Hill, Wandsworth, was very fortuitous, as owners departed downhill and if any troubles developed they had to get up again to protest. This hill was a tram-route and used sunken power cables, and the trams got their power by means of a trailing power conductor. One day a GN lost one of its chains down this gap and all the trams stopped in their tracks.

J.C. Vredenburg had taken over Wilkinson's shares after the war. He had got to know Nash when his wife had been in the nursing home at The Elms run by Nash's mother, and in the new company there were also directors from the British Gregoire Co. Monsieur Marcel Lourde was a director of British Gregoire, and he negotiated with the Société des Moteurs Salmson, at Billancourt near Paris, for them to build the GN under licence in France and sell it under the name of GN. Drawings were sent over in 1919. By the time of the Paris Salon they had produced six cars, much to Nash and Godfrey's surprise. They flew to Paris in Nash's Avro 504K, and Nash's passport had 'par air si possible' written in by a disbelieving civil servant. Both of them were highly impressed with the finish of the GN, as shown at the Salon, and they borrowed one of the cars to drive it around Paris to see how good it was. On their return to the Salon, the car was surrounded by an admiring crowd, and Nash stood up in the seat and shouted: 'Vive la France – clear out of the way, you baskets.'

It was fortunate that this agreement was made, for in May 1920 the French government prohibited the import of motor vehicles. Salmsons had been aero engine manufacturers, producing certainly more than 1,500 aero engines and later upwards of 2,000 GNs. In 1922 they produced their first four-cylinder car, which in its design had a number of GN chassis features, and was the first car they made to bear the name Salmson. The GN was the father of all the French light sports cars. In total, Salmsons paid GN £15,500 in fees and royalties.

This was the high point in GN's existence; they were making as many cars as they could possibly manufacture at the East Hill works, and, far more important, were selling them. A steadily growing export market and Salmson's operations in France and in their export territories emphasised their strength. A special engine was made at this time with a long stroke and small bore which was known on the works drawings as the 6.3 ATM. The ATM was a 'derisive anatomical gesture to the then Chancellor of the Exchequer, McKenna.'

Motor-racing started again in 1919, and Brooklands reopened in 1920. Nash started to race with 'Kim', and in his first appearance with the car at a JCC meeting won every race for which he was entered. The car, for its capacity, had a startling performance, being able to get

In August 1920 – Archie Nash crashed Kim at Brooklands.

up to 85mph coming off the banking, and was unquestionably the fastest 1,100cc racing car in the world in 1920. At the BARC meeting on August the second, Nash got into a spin, having been caught in the slipstream of a faster car, and Kim went off the track backwards, going very fast indeed. He had earlier learned another valuable lesson from one other spin; a hand throttle had been fitted; as the bumping at Brooklands made it very difficult to keep a constant foot pressure. When the car went into a spin he found it impossible to close the hand throttle – subsequently the hand throttles were spring-loaded to the closed position.

Archie Nash was lucky to have escaped with his life from that accident, as it was he did not race again that season, but he did break the records up to 1,500cc for standing and flying half-mile, kilometre and mile with a best flying speed of 86.29mph. He had also obtained FTD at South Harting Hill-Climb. GN entered three cars in the Land's End Trial and they all won gold medals, the only team to do so. On one occasion, Nash was parked in Kim at the side of the road in Bexhill on his way to a hill-climb when a horseman going in the opposite direction shouted ruderies at him. Nash slipped into reverse and passed the derisory horseman going flat out in reverse up to 50mph (the centrifugal Smith's speedometer of that time would read in reverse) and this performance became known as the 'World's land speed record in reverse'.

For the 1921 season Kim was rebuilt into Kim II, the pre-war ash chassis had been replaced by a new 1920 chassis, which was much drilled for lightness, but the same body was repaired and put back. Kim II became as unbeatable as Kim had been. It was a tremendous competition year for GN, as they gained 112 firsts at speed trials and a considerable number of FTDs. Kim II was unbeatable, except oddly at Shelsley. When Nash was not competing, Godfrey often won on Bluebottle. Bluebottle was a 1914 Vitesse GN, with an ash frame and belt drive, and fitted with an engine that had the same bottom-end as Kim's engine. It was built from

Kim's engine lying on the floor of Ron Godfrey's barn where it lay from 1922 until the 1950s.

Kim is rebuilt as Kim II with a conventional steering box, wire and bobbin being deemed obsolete. The car, with Archie (his hands are just visible) behind the wheel, has the hood up and a celluloid screen. He is ready to set off up the A1 to Skegness in 1921.

the parts rescued after the war, from the second engine made for the abandoned 1914 Isle of Man race.

Nash had, by the 1921 season, got the racing bug badly – it was quite possible to have a one-sided conversation with him when his mind was obviously elsewhere. Whenever his eyes became glazed, he was said in the works to have gained the 90mph look. Early in 1921 the JCC announced that a 200-mile race was to be run at Brooklands in October for cars of up to 1,500cc capacity. H.J. Morgan wrote of the 200-Mile race in the foreword to Boddy's excellent book of that name: 'The "two hundred" was something so new and ambitious that it overshadowed all past achievements. This race, incidentally, was the first long-distance event ever to be organised in this country… All sorts of fearsome results were promised by the hoodoo experts when the race was first mooted.'

The race was to be run in two separate sections: 1,100cc and 1,500cc cars. One entry was made by GN Ltd for Nash to drive. The intention was to use Mowgli, the car having been entered in the August 1921 Boulogne Week. There was an excellent racing department in the works, though for political reasons it was called the Experimental Shop. In the 1,100cc section, Lombard in the Salmson led Nash for half the race, but the Salmson's extended refuelling stop put Nash firmly in the lead and he won the class at an average speed of 71.54mph and with a fuel consumption of 33mpg. On the last lap he recorded 77.45mph to show that the GN had as much in hand as Segrave had in the Darracq to win the 1,500cc class.

Nash drove this same car in the 1922 200-Mile Race, and two cars were driven by Godfrey and a very enthusiastic chauffeur named Hawkins, who drove Pickett's car. Pickett, the uncrowned armament's 'King of Boulogne', being his employer. Godfrey's and Hawkins' ohc drive was a straight shaft mounted on the cylinder barrel line. Nash's engine was by now a bit long in the tooth, since he had used it several times at Brooklands in the intervening year, and in the race a piston collapsed. No doubt Len Cushman was not too unhappy at the forty-two-minute break afforded by the piston collapsing as he could arise from his mattress to help in the stripping down of a barrel and head to fit a new piston. H.J. Aldington said many years later:

> *Frazer-Nash, as well as being a gifted engineer, was a superlative mechanic. I have seen him strip down engines in the middle of a race without even turning up his shirt cuffs, and when the work was done only his fingers would be dirty. Not for nothing was he a first-class Board of Trade inspector; he had a marvellous eye for just looking at a mechanical object and telling whether it was right or wrong.*

Late in 1920 GN began to feel the backwash of the end of the post-war boom, which affected all car manufacturers, and cyclecar manufacturers in particular. GNs were not being sold as fast as they were being made. A receiver, McClintock, was appointed, and in 1921 a Mr Black bought out the control of the company, forming GN Motors Ltd. Norman Black, his son, became the sales manager of the company and a major policy decision was taken which proved to be a mistake. Having got into mass-production, the directors were reluctant to lose this part of the market; Godfrey and Nash argued that it would be better to develop the GN as a sports car and forget about mass-production. They were overruled.

Raymond Morgan wrote in a *Chain-Gang Gazette* of 1962:

> *One of the fascinating things about the GN was its extraordinary assembly of noises, and it was not at all uncommon for somebody to ring up and say, 'I have got a new noise like so-and-so.*

The T-drive shaft ohc engine for the 1921 200-Mile Race.

Mrs Graunch has got no worse, and the sisters Plinket are about the same as usual, but this is quite different,' and the owner would then go on to describe, using all sorts of not always refined analogies, what the noise sounded like, and often they were recognisable as being symptoms of this, that or the other. One thing that was nice about the GN, which was not common to many cars was the peculiar 'three-to-five chaplonk', which came from the 90-degree engine; plus the combination of different sounds from the Graunches and sisters Plinket. It was said that Archie's bulldog was always able to detect Archie's car by its sound from the other GNs.

Nash was asked why they did not improve the silencers on the standard GN. He pointed out that this would make the other noises more noticeable. The racing GNs were noisy but so were the touring models, and this became obvious at the 1921 Olympia Show where there was a demonstration car to take prospective purchasers around the back streets. Wilkinson, who was the chief demonstrator, was not insensitive to the high noise level. On one occasion he remarked to a potential buyer: 'What are you complaining about, you have only been in the car five minutes whilst I have to put up with it all day.'

At the end of 1921 the groundswell of complaints from the agents had arisen, due to the signs of the slump that was coming. The following items of complaint were raised: the engine to be more silent; the body to be more comfortable; and a better technical specification. Everybody agreed about the noisiness of the GN engine. The range of noises were legion: valve gear noise, piston slap, etc. There was no part of the engine that did not add its own contribution to the orchestration; to fit more efficient silencers would have made the 'cha-plinks' and 'cha-plunks' of the valve train even more noticeable.

The coachwork that had been fitted to the 1914 GN had seemed at that time to be the last word, especially when fitted with a windscreen and hood – though by 1921 it was regarded as primitive. The absence of a door in the specification meant that the body frame could be light, simple and cheap to produce. Archie Nash was resolutely opposed to a door as the whole body had to be stiffened up to take it, and to one prospective customer who enquired about a door, he said: 'Door, door, what do you want with a door?' Nash and Godfrey saw no reason why any changes at all should be made to such a fine car, but they were fully receptive to suggestions for mechanical improvement; for instance, that a device could be used on the hub-nuts to stop the nut unscrewing, which would prevent the wheels falling off. They were not at all receptive to suggestions that the GN should be made more like a car than a cyclecar; this they felt was not merited, since there was supplied with each post-war car a well designed and manufactured hood and a spare wheel with its own mounting bracket.

The GN might be raised to a higher specification through improved technical standards, for example, making electric lighting more of a fitting than an extra and adding instruments – 'what do they want an oil gauge for, when there is no pressure to be read?' The partners also recognised that the side starting handle was out of date and front starting was required. Unfortunately, however, due to the overhung crank design it meant that the extension to the crankshaft used for the valve gear operation was not robust enough to be cranked around by the energetic use of a starting handle.

From the beginning in 1911, there had been an extension to the counter shaft from the bevel box, with which a starting handle could engage sticking out just behind the driver's seat; the car could be hand, or kick-started and a hand throttle mounted to the side of the bodywork could mean that the engine could be encouraged to keep on firing after the first firing stroke. It was simple and straightforward, but by the early 1920s people did not expect

The GN stand at the 1921 Motor Show with a front starting handle car fitted with a door.

to see a starting handle fed into the middle of a car. Many people, always ready to laugh at the bizarre, laughed at the GN side starting. Nash said to Orrinsmith, who was the chief draughtsman, 'When I come in tomorrow I want to see a design on my desk, which means we can get away from the side starting handle'. Orrinsmith's note on Nash's desk the next morning stated simply 'problem insoluble, cars will have to be sold, started'. The problem was eventually solved, but the result was more expensive to manufacture, involved poor engineering in stiffening up the valve gear train and was likely to cause trouble before the cars were very old.

The car was redesigned to provide more comfort. A door was incorporated into the body on the passenger's side, the body made wider and the engine de-tuned to reduce the noise level. Nash and Godfrey recognised that the requests from agents asking for improvements to be made, to uplift the GN specification to that of a light car, had the fatal drawback that the price had, according to the agents, to remain at that of a cyclecar.

The 1922 models, as they were called, were introduced in late 1921 and modified the performance to an almost pedestrian level so that cars under favourable conditions could only just obtain 40mph. This was the kiss of death. In 1922 another desperate decision was taken and that was to market a shaft-drive, four-cylinder, water-cooled car. The prototype was built and did many thousands of miles around the roads. So as not to suggest that the older GNs were doomed, and not to compete with the chain-driven cars, the name of Steiner was on the radiator. The Steiner was powered by a DFP engine – Godfrey had been to the Ardennes, in France, and had a demonstration in a car powered with one of these engines. He liked the engine and recommended its use. The shaft-driven car was the final death struggle. In April 1922, a second receiver was appointed and the shaft-drive cars finally got into production at the end of that year. The directors had in the meantime opted for the cheaper French CIME engine to be fitted.

The basic trouble at East Hill was that production had not really commenced until the end of 1920 and there had been too short a time to start paying back the capital investment. If East Hill had been in production a year earlier, then the two senior partners would have had their way when things started to go wrong. They wished at the end of 1921 to cut back production and move into the sports car market, where most of the disadvantages of the design could have been made into advantages, and where there could have been room for manoeuvre on pricing when changes were required. The point of view which envisaged a reduction in output, was an anathema to the Board of GN who, other than Nash and Godfrey, were British Gregoire appointees and they thought that it was agreed that all that was best in British light cars was to be seen in the Rover 8. It was grudgingly agreed that a Rover 8 would be examined throughout and all those features that could be incorporated, should be incorporated in a completely new model. In the meantime, some changes would be introduced into the 1922 range to create a halfway stage. These would incorporate most of the suggestions that were being made by the agents. Greater width bodies with a door were to be the standard, and the 1922 catalogue in its preamble stated the following: 'COMFORT. Only when a car is well-proportioned, quiet and sweet running can comfort be attained. The 1922 GN is roomy, luxuriously comfortable, gives perfect protection in any weather; its chassis, too, is as excellent as its bodywork is beautiful.' After this preamble the 1922 potential purchaser could not have been surprised by the first page of the text which stated that the 'All-Weather Model' was, by inference, a beautiful car.

A brand new Légère model with a polished aluminium skin and fitted with electric lights as all GNs were from the beginning of 1920.

The 1922 GN had a front-starting handle which predetermined a flat 'radiator' front. This is the De Luxe model photographed on August Bank Holiday Monday 1921, with three members of the manufacturing staff in their 'best'.

It was not until the last few pages of this catalogue were reached, that from two whole pages of small type, it could be seen that the GN was a very successful competition car. A GN had won the Tourist Championship of France, as the catalogue said, 'the highest obtainable class award of the continent', and a whole page of racing successes, not only class awards but many Fastest Time of the Day awards, were listed. It also featured a remarkable ninety-four miles to the gallon recorded during the Midland Light Car Club's one-day road trial that included the Old Wyche Cutting at Malvern with a gradient of 1 in 3.

One of the features of the 1922 range was that the engines had been modified to lower the noise level. The chief modification was to the design of the cams, which meant that in quietening the ramps, the power of the engine was seriously reduced. When this was compounded with the increased weight of the coachwork, the original performance, which had been positively sporting by the standards of the time, dropped to a more pedestrian level, and the fuel consumption was markedly worse. The Grand Prix GN of 1914 always gave 60mpg, the immediate post-war cars gave at least 45mpg, with an easy 55mpg obtainable on a long run, but the 1922 car was at its best a 40-45mpg car.

The strain of what was happening in the works in 1922 was more than Archie Nash could stand, practically every change that had been made from the last quarter onwards from 1921 had been specifically against his advice. In most cases he had not only argued against the change but would have preferred a change, if it had to be made, to be in the diametrically opposite direction. In all cases Ron Godfrey agreed with Nash, but was not as vocal in his disagreement. The increased capital they had to take on in 1920 meant that the senior partners now held only a minority shareholding. The 1922 models, when designed, were against Nash and Godfrey's judgement but they co-operated in the implementation of the Board's decision; they realised that they could be wrong, and that what the market was looking for were the 1922 Touring and All-Weather models. In fact, they were not wrong and sales were poor even in relation to the end of 1921. The Board in 1922 decided to carry on with the development of the 1923 car, the Steiner. Nash argued that to carry on with this was suicide, but it was too late for the Board to turn round and admit its mistakes and Nash resigned and left the company. Ron Godfrey thought he could stick it out, but with his partner and friend gone, he could only stand it for a month and by the autumn of 1922 he also resigned. The board of GN Ltd recognised Archie's input to the success of GN and arranged for him to receive a monthly emolument. He had been receiving £86 6s 8d monthly as a director. This was replaced with an attractive agreement as to his having the free usage of racing parts and obsolete parts, plus a monthly cash payment of £29 3s 4d while he built up the Frazer Nash car.

The 1923 GN was in essence a side-valve Rover 8 with the cylinders at ninety degrees instead of the Rover's 180 degrees. It is likely that an agreement was struck with Salmson to purchase in their GN developed components, probably via Hinstin who seemingly had taken over the GN from Salmson. The overhung crankshaft design had gone and the advertisement from *The Motor Cycle*, of October 1922, shows the changes which, as *The Light Car and Cyclecar* pointed out, were revolutionary. For GN to abandon chain drive was revolutionary. There was not a single component in the car that had not been changed – even parts such as the front axle and steering box had been unnecessarily modified, even if outwardly they looked the same. Some of the replacement components were undoubtedly French, but many items were new and of British manufacture. The four-cylinder car was less than satisfactory and the minimum-priced model at 205 guineas, reduced in December to the more plebeian £195, compared unfavourably with the Rover 8, selling at £180. The press said that 'the new vee-twin engine is particularly silent', but this did not compensate for only a trickle of orders. The guarantee claims, especially on the CIME four-cylinder engined model, were very high.

The firm and the cars were in the throes of death and the unkindest cut of all was that *The Light Car and Cyclecar*, both in the readers' letters and the editorial, seldom referred to the new GN models. The comments in the correspondence columns were warmly disposed to the older models, references were made to the economy and, as one correspondent wrote, 'as for the chain drive I can only wonder why the makers departed from it'. An article on the merits of four-cylinder cars against twin cylinder cars compared the two new GN models in March of 1923, where the writer noted ironically and, as he said, with 'lingering regret', that 'no longer was there the typical bark for which the GN was famous.'

October 1922 was a sad month. Both Godfrey and Nash had left the company and the new models were announced. Chain-drive cars were no longer listed. All that was available were two shaft-drive cars, one with a vee-twin GN engine, coupled to a three-speed gearbox and the other the four-cylinder, water-cooled engine. The substitution of the cheaper CIME engine, rather than the DFP, led to endless troubles, and the guarantee claims finally completely bankrupted the company.

May 1923 was the finish of GN Motors Ltd. The Monthly Trade Review of that month reported that a meeting of creditors and shareholders of GN Motors Ltd was to be held on Monday, 2 July, at which a liquidator would be appointed. The salient reasons for the failure, all of which were a little bit true but not the whole truth, were listed – among these was 'the engineers' lock-out in 1922'. The deficiency in regard to the shareholders was reported as being over £84,000. However, Pearson, who was the manager of the repair shop, got together with Walter Laffan and formed a new company, GN Ltd, to provide servicing and spares for the older models. Lewington, in the service department, drew up an analysis of the previous year's turnover of spares and repairs. These figures were £10,272 for spares and £7,593 for repairs, totalling £17,865 for the year. Earnings for the first four months of 1923 totalled £5,283. The total for the whole of 1922 was £6,950 profit for this side of the business. Lewington's report made several points as to why the profitability should improve, notably all work on directors' cars and competition would not be recurring and that the figures for 1923 are better than at first appear 'since the amount of work guaranteed has been extraordinarily heavy.'

In 1924 and 1925 a few old chain-drive chassis were assembled with the Anzani 11.9 engine, but Walter Laffan softened the springs and put more camber on them. On cornering these springs tended to flatten, causing gross over-steer; this car was not a success.

In 1929 GN spares were being sold out at scrap prices, and the Clayton Mineral Water Co. took over the East Hill Works; the new firm of GN Ltd became a garage and acquired a dealership for General Motors' products. Godfrey, in 1923, founded H.R. Godfrey (GN spares and repairs). He got a contract to maintain and overhaul the sixty or so GNs owned by the Cherry Blossom Boot Polish Co., which their travellers used. This was good bread-and-butter business, for no sooner was the servicing of the fleet completed, than it needed to be started again. Stuart Proctor joined Godfrey. They had access to many tons of GN parts, and they evolved several cars that used combinations of GN and Austin 7 parts. According to Ron Godfrey, the best of them was a GN chassis with an Austin 7 engine, GN clutch and chain-drive with Austin 7 brakes to the front axle. In 1927, part of the garage at Manor Road, Richmond, was let out to H.J. Aldington to found Aldington Motors. In the mid-1930s, Godfrey helped to found the HRG car with Proctor.

Nash and Godfrey never had to rationalise their desire to go motor racing, there never was any question to them whether they would be improving the breed. It was clear that if one competed, the standards of manufacture improved, the cars got better and the public bought the cars. If none of this had been true, however, they would have still gone motor racing, because it was fun, and business without fun was not what they wanted before the First World War. After the war the situation was different, since they then employed over 500 people and responsibility allied with the money conscious other directors of GN, meant that they had to make a case out for competition.

In the post-war period they had to go motor racing because there was no more effective way of demonstrating their wares and thereby selling them. Even as the troubles of the company became overwhelming, the competition department at the East Hill Works was producing racing cars and many sports racing variations of the vee-twin engine.

The Streamer was the first racing car built by the firm, being a single-seater version of the 1912 car. In 1912 there was a plethora of large single-cylinder engines on the market, notably the De Dion. Godfrey was not averse to buying these for next to nothing and driving them hard in a GN chassis on the Hendon Test Track, to see if lessons could be learned. The test track at the Hendon Works, sounding very impressive, was a circle of hard packed earth of about 40-50 yards in diameter behind Archie's mothers house.

The Grand Prix GN, though neither a single-seater nor a racing car entirely, was built for the 1913 Amiens Race and was the forebear of all later cars.

1. The definition of a cyclecar and microcar, for the purpose of this book, is that they use the technology of the pedal-cycle or motorcycle in its design. Very few cyclecars came up the pedal-cycle route; the exceptions being the Guyot-Mochon in France and the Briggs and Stratton in the States. (Peter Harper collection)

2. An impression by Gamy of a 1912 period Bédélia together with a further French period piece (3).

4. GN were to produce a 1914 catalogue with this painting on the cover depicting the GN in the 1914 Cyclecar GP at Amiens. The outbreak of the Great War made this catalogue still-born. The significant difference from the 1913 entry was to be the stone guard in front of the engine.

5. A detail of the artwork produced by Ernst Deutsch (later known as Ernst Dryden, when living in the US in the 1930s) for the German magazine Die Dame at the end of the 1920s. The buckboard is a Red Bug driven by a battery-powered electric motor. The Red Bugs were built in the United States, developed from the Briggs & Stratton's buckboard design. Note the electric-powered klaxon. Examples of these buckboards were still common at Deauville and Le Touquet in the early 1950s.

£165

THE

1921

"TAMPLIN"

Four-
Wheeler

£165

6. Left: *The front cover of the Tamplin brochure of 1921.*

7 & 8. Below: *The Tamplin incorporated a name plate on the front and had slightly different rear body work. It had a staggered driver's seat, like the Carden, so that the rear seat passenger could stretch his legs forward. (Peter Harper collection)*

9. *The Manchester-built Harper. (Peter Harper collection)*

10. *A Carden with the traditional black 'radiator' and no name plate.*

11 & 12. A Spacke engine was fitted to a Spacke shipped to Sweden in 1921; it was of 1918 construction and fitted with the forty-five-degree angle engine and Atwater-Kent distributor, powered by a trembler coil.

13. H.M. Bateman was a noted cartoonist from the 1920s forward and this was printed in the Tatler, November 1927 (only the detail with the Morgan is shown). It is captioned, 'The car that touched a Policeman'.

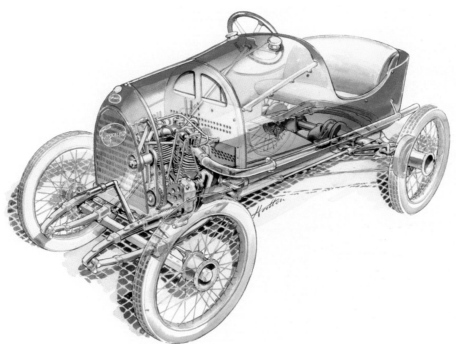

14. An Italian Temperino of the 1920s, made in Turin with a one-litre Della Ferrari engine, which drove a back axle gearbox and only the offside wheel. (The Autocar and Motor archive)

15 & 16. *The late 1922 GN catalogue promoting the 1923 GNs. It is now believed that this car was probably made by Hinstin in Maubeuge, France, for the 1922 owners of GN. Certainly there is not a single component on the car which is the same as the 1922 cars – though at first glance some might appear to have an affinity – notably the steering box.*

17. Left: *The four-cylinder GN was styled on the Rover 8. An extra was a self starter 'if so desired'.*

*18. Above is an advertisement from
October 1926.*

*19. Left: The word 'Runabout' was not
a model name, but encompassed the
whole of the Morgan range.*

20. A Scott Sociable, the property of the Bradford Industrial Museum.

21. The 1957 BMW Isetta 600, with a 582cc engine was an upmarket move from the front opening 300. The spare wheel was located in the front door – a primitive air-bag? An additional door at the rear provided access to the two rear seats.

22. *Maico manufactured motor cycles from 1932. In 1955 they took over the rights to the Champion which had been the brain child of a former BMW engineer, Hermann Holbein, whose first microcar design dated back to 1946. The Maico 500 made between 1956 and 1958 was fitted with a 450cc twin-cylinder two-stroke engine.*

23. *The 250/ 300/400 Goggomobil Regent.*

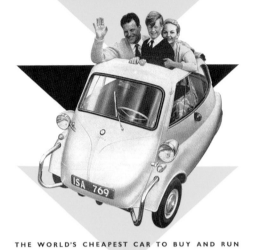

THE WORLD'S CHEAPEST CAR TO BUY AND RUN

Built at Brighton, Sussex

24. *An advertisement for the Brighton-built Isetta.*

EVERY INCH A REAL CAR!

25. *The Berkeley T60 three wheeler was introduced in August 1959 and soon became the most successful Berkeley model.*

26. A Heinkel, photographed in Sweden in 1993.

27. Messerschmitt Kr175 at Hopetoun House, West Lothian. Fitted is the optional suitcase rack.

28. *Stella Fitzgerald in a Peel P50 – the smallest production single seat car in the world.*

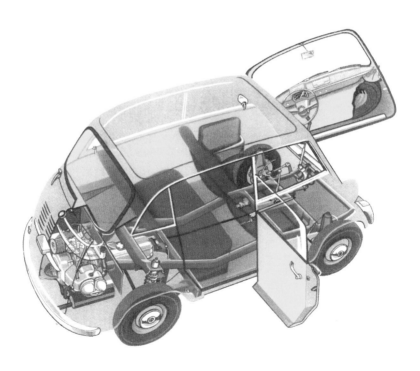

29. *A colour cutaway of a BMW 600 from an advertising brochure.*

30 & 31. *The Bond Minicar Mark C and Mark G.*

32 & 33. The cyclecar is not yet dead. The Vespa Ape (above) uses the transmission and engine of a Vespa Scooter, whilst the more recent Piaggio Ape has to work with a 50cc engine.

The three GNs entered for the 1922 200-Mile Race at Brooklands run down to the start, with Cushman about to submerge onto his mattress. To the far left is the AV Bicar, driven by Avey, which succeeded the monocar for AV. Behind are the three twin-cam Salmsons.

GN never forsook the overhung crank where the crankshaft was held in position external to the body of the crankcase and sump in an extension. The overhung crank could be made using only a lathe as the production piece of machinery. Kim's engine, an overhead valve development of the GN engine, was designed for the Isle of Man International Cyclecar Race, to be known as the Dangerfield Trophy, after the Managing Director of Temple Press. It was intended to be the British equivalent of the Amiens race. This trophy was to be raced over a ten-lap course from St Johns to Kirkmichael, to Peel and returning to St Johns giving a lap of almost sixteen miles. The regulations for the 1914 TT acted as a catalyst on Nash and Godfrey in the same way as the Amiens GP had done for the GP GN. The result of the chemistry was Kim. The race was to take place on 24 September 1914, and by mid-July the new GN, Kim, weighing only 3½cwt, was entered and ready, but on its first appearance it was beaten by Carden in a single-seater Carden.

Kim's engine was the first attempt by the firm to produce a racing engine. The 90-bore overhead valve JAP engine used in the racing Morgans was the spur, as prior to the First World War, these engines gave 30hp-plus. The standard Inlet over Exhaust GN engine was in the 16-18bhp class. The exploits of Kim and Kim II from 1913 to 1922 were incredible. It is probably true to say that no other engined car has held so many records in so short a time. Kim was easily the fastest 1,100cc racing car before the War and probably the fastest car in the world up to 80mph, the all-up weight being only 3½cwt.

The aluminium cast crankcase was very much stiffer than any GN engine previously. The cast iron bolted-on crankcase extension held the crankshaft external to the sump. The rigidity of not only the crankshaft, but the whole engine, was considerably better. Kim's engine was fitted with ball and roller bearings throughout. The works had built their first out and out racing engine.

Kim's heads were cast in bronze, with some difficulty – and although the heads are referred to as being bronze, these were actually cast in a brass used in marine work for superheated steam cocks. The metal did not flow cleanly. Difficulty in getting the metal to flow probably displaced the core in one case and the thickness of metal in one head is as little as $\frac{1}{16}$in. This was checked by drilling a small hole and later plugging it. No trouble was subsequently ever experienced in these thin walled heads. The heads had two valves with valve heads 2ins diameter set at ninety degrees.

Kim II was found to be considerably faster on recorded lap speeds, after the rebuild following Archie's crash. The racing staff of GN discussed the reason; it was Godfrey who realised that it had to be that the rebuilt car had less rolling resistance. Archie Nash decided that racing cars go better after a crash as the car had been stress relieved! The outcome of this entertaining surmise was that a test was instituted on a very slight downward slope by the hut that GN rented at Brooklands. GNs were released without a driver aboard, where they stopped, some ten yards further on, a peg duly annotated to the car and its condition on the day was placed in the grass at the side of the road. For cars of identical weight a great deal of care was taken to reduce the differences. They found that the two-seater cars tended to roll only a small increment farther and so, after a year of these tests, all the stakes were clustered together and the test became known to the GN people as 'The Flying Millimetre'.

Kim was primarily designed as a sprint and hill climb machine in which it excelled. Development never stands still and it was in 1919 that Godfrey and Nash set about designing a more powerful and elaborate engine which would stand up to long periods of full throttle round Brooklands. Mowgli, the single-seater GN, had this engine installed. It was a complete breakaway from normal GN practice, but still retained the overhung crank.

The crankcase of aluminium was cast with a deep square sump with cooling fins. At the rear was the cast iron mainshaft, bearing housing carrying the shaft in roller and ball bearings, similar to Kim. The built-up crankshaft now had a roller crank pin and three tracks of $\frac{3}{8}$in rollers, twelve per track, upon which ran the two rods, one forked and one plain. The timing

The 1922 style of the Akela engines with the camshaft drive up the front of the barrels. The cast iron extension holding the overhung crankshaft and the standard GN steering box can be seen.

case carried the half time gear wheel which drove the overhead camshafts by exposed roller chain through a system of sprockets. The cylinders were normal cast iron set as usual at ninety degrees. The pistons were aluminium with two rings. The cylinder heads were bronze with pent roof heads each fitted with four valves. Over each cylinder head was mounted a large aluminium cambox carrying a four-cam camshaft in ball bearings. The valves were driven by four separate rockers, the ends of which engaged in slotted tappets running in bronze bushes.

Mowgli's engine had the single chain-driven camshaft set in front of the cylinders origi-nally. This was altered later to drive up the rear of the cylinders. This engine was run with much success in Mowgli, but from time to time was beset with camshaft chain trouble. The chain drive ohc models being known as the 'chainmaker's delight', engaged the driving sprocket at a very wide angle, thereby coming into contact with only three teeth at a time. The short chassis of Kim was too twitchy at high speeds with side winds, so a new chassis was developed with the standard back axle made into a countershaft and a further axle, the back axle driven by a single chain, added. This created a car of approximately 10ft wheelbase and Mowgli was the given name. Kim's engine was often fitted. Mowgli's engine, which went on to power Basil Davenport's Spider, was highly successful in obtaining British national records, but on long distance events the camshaft drive system, on several occasions, let the car down. Nevertheless, the works persisted in this drive with its single 6ft run of roller chain. The engine could be run in three guises, as the standard 84mm x 98mm (1,086cc), or 89mm x 98mm (1,219cc), or 89mm x120mm (1,493cc) – in the last two of these categories it was used only for record breaking attempts. The difficulty with the chain drive was not that necessarily of the drive, but of the limited number of teeth that took the drive from the crankshaft and the limited number of teeth that were in mesh for the magneto drive. To prevent the chain jumping, it had to be heavily tensioned. Why two such inventive engineers as Nash and Godfrey persisted with this design when, with only the smallest modification, they could have had two separate chains driving the camshafts to give a more than adequate chain wrap around the sprockets, and a short, third chain driving the magneto, is difficult to understand. GN never produced an engine with a single chain to each camshaft, it was left to amateur owners and drivers that followed them to introduce this simple design change.

The 1921 Boulogne meeting brought home to them the deficiency of the design. The sprint course and the Boulogne Grand Prix course involved the use of the road from Boulogne to Le Wast, with its continuous up and downhill roller-coaster gradient, where the revolutions the engine could reach in top gear were described as 'the like of which had never been seen before'! The camshaft drive chain gave continuous trouble and even tightening up to a board-like configuration gave no remedy, with the chain breaking due to over tension.

The time between the 1921 Boulogne race and the October 200-Mile Race at Brooklands was about three months and in that time they built the Akela engine, with shaft and bevel gear camshaft drive.

The original Akela was aptly named – Akela was Kipling's lone wolf. The engine was in fact a development of Mowgli, using the same crankshaft arrangement, except that the timing chest was much modified, so as to accept a better design of flycrank housing and the bevel drive to the vertical-camshaft drive. All these drives used splines, so that the problems of expansion and contraction could be overcome. The cylinder heads were a highly advanced pent-roof design of bronze with four valves and two sparking plugs. Three similar bronze castings were used, one for the bottom bevel and one for each cambox. The first was placed centrally in the steel front plate and drove through a splined bevel, a vertical shaft set midway between the two centre lines of the camshafts. This shaft terminated in a bevel, which drove a half-time bevel enclosed in a miniature GN bevel box. The horizontal shaft mated up with the two cambox bevel boxes; all bevels except the 2:1 gearbox bevels ran on splined shafts.

The general appearance of the camshaft drive suggested an upraised arm and this was christened the 'I Swear' engine by Orrinsmith, since it reminded him of filmed court room scenes where the witness raised his clenched fist. This engine later became known as the 'T' camshaft Akela and is the only GN engine built by the firm to use single blade connecting rods on the overhung crank. These ran side by side on two rows of $\frac{3}{8}$in rollers on a short crankpin. As the cylinders were not staggered the little ends were offset in the gudgeon pin bosses.

Godfrey and Nash confirmed that this was the fastest Akela engine made in the 1,086cc size, although later on this also was opened out to 1,200cc and 1,500cc similar to Mowgli's. Mowgli in the 1,200cc size just failed to lap Brooklands at 90mph driven by Archie. He never drove these engines at much more than 3,500rpm as this was considered the maximum speed for reliability at the time. Basil Davenport, when he first acquired the 1,500cc Mowgli in 1923–1924, raised the compression ratio and found it revolved happily at 5,000rpm, but with doubtful reliability, due to flexing of the overhung crank, which bent the forked big end eventually leading to fracture just above the con rod fork.

The complexity of drive and the sophistication of the whole engine design showed that, though the firm was in business making cyclecars, they were not going to compromise on the design of the engine for the 200-Mile Race. This race from the time it was proposed had excited the imaginations of the light car manufacturers, in the same manner as had the 1913 Amiens Cyclecar Grand Prix in earlier years.

The single GN entry for the 1,100cc class of the 1921 200-Mile Race was driven by Archie Nash with Cushman as his riding mechanic, and they won the class. Cushman should have been awarded a cup. Nash had noticed that the regulations did not say that the passenger need be sitting up, or as Cushman dryly noted 'even alive', and he lay prone on a mattress unable to bodily resist Brookland's bumps.

During the early months of 1922, reconsideration was given to sports-racing and racing engines. The 1921 developments with the T Akela engine and the chain-driven overhead camshaft Vitesse engine were the prototypes for the 1922 season. The Akela engine was redesigned to have a single-shaft drive to the overhead camshafts, up the line of the barrels, similar to the classic layout of 'cammy' Velocettes and Manx Nortons, but in GN vernacular the new Akela engines were also known as the vee-drive engines. The T Akela engine had introduced side by side connecting rods and it was therefore a surprise that the vee-camshaft engines reverted to the traditional forked and plain connecting rod arrangement. The works engines rarely exceeded 3,500rpm and failures in rods, whilst the firm was active, were almost unheard of.

There was always a terrible tendency to prove a car over and over again. Inevitably, by the time a race came around, the car would be worn out! Archie was a good listener and could be tempted to introduce design changes too late for them to be adequately tested. In the 1922 200-mile event, Nash decided at the last minute, as he would be entered in the 1921 car, to try out some experimental pistons. The race started splendidly with Nash averaging 78.78mph for a standing start fifty mile record, with Cushman lying beside him for the second successive year – shortly after this a piston collapsed. Nash and Cushman changed the piston in 42 minutes, which was excellent going, and they still finished the race, at an average speed of 62mph. The Salmson team were miles an hour faster than the GN, however, and had averaged 81.88mph to win. Godfrey, Hawkins & Nash finished third, fourth and fifth to the Salmsons, and they also won the Team Prize.

They did produce a few sports racing engines using plate drives that are now legends. This type of camshaft drive was known in the works as the 'Duke of Argyll drive'. The drive was taken up the line of the barrels and across the heads, making a triangulated series of off-centre plates with counter balancing bobweights. It was known as the Duke of Argyll drive as the Duke of that time had had installed rubbing posts for his cattle in his fields, and as the cows dropped their shoulders to rub against the posts they produced a strange off-centre motion with the top of their bodies, while keeping their feet still. This sometimes led those not 'in the know' to believe that the Duke was in some way involved in the affairs of GN.

In 1921 the firm had experimented with a half way design of engine, intended as a sports racer and was indicative of the direction that Godfrey and Nash thought was the way for the firm to go. The simple Vitesse engine of 1919, with its push rod operated overhead valves, was to be supplanted with an engine that would be cheap to build but with chain driven overhead camshafts, as advanced a design as any engine on the market. The prototype running in 1921 had a bronze nearside and cast iron offside cylinder heads but by 1922 they were both made in iron. A perfectly formed hemispherical cylinder head with twin valves coupled with a crankcase and crankshaft of Akela standard was of an advanced enough design to satisfy anybody and it was also remarkably cheap to build in quantity. The whole history of the GN company is plagued with 'might have beens', but if the company had produced sports racing GNs, powered with such an engine, rather than tourers in 1922 then it is difficult not to believe that the market that Morgan was building up would not have also been open to GN.

Ruby Aldington, wife of W.H. Aldington, who was later to be the marketing man for Frazer Nash cars, with a 1922 GN with the front-starting handle.

Ron Godfrey and Archie Frazer-Nash were honoured by Temple Press (publishers of Light Car and Cyclecar*) at a special luncheon party at the Connaught Rooms, which over seventy people attended in February 1948 to honour the memory of the GN. Leslie Wilson, the then secretary for the Midland Automobile Club, stands between them. (MAC Archive)*

Showing the roomy body and dickey seat of the Standard Model.

THE FOUR CYLINDER G.N

The four-cylinder GN was styled on the Rover 8. An extra was a self starter 'if so desired'.

3
The Morgan

The Morgan was the best known of the British three-wheelers and has to rank as the most successful cyclecar built in the world. It was in production as a vee-twin engined car with final chain transmission from 1910 until 1946. The lower horsepower tax for three-wheelers gave them a distinct financial advantage over their four-wheeled brethren.

Harry Morgan, always known as HFS, bought an Eagle Tandem three-wheeler in 1901. It was tricar, or forecar, with the passenger seated between the two front wheels. HFS went into business in a garage in Malvern Link in Worcestershire. The two brothers Stephenson-Peach were friends of Harry Morgan, and through them HFS met the senior Stephenson-Peach who was a master at Malvern College and in charge of the Engineering/Technical department. English public schools that had an engineering facility and background were, and are, extremely rare – with Malvern there were Eton, Wellington, Repton and Oundle and Bedford College.

HFS, by 1909, with Stephenson-Peach, had constructed the first Morgan three-wheeler in the Malvern College workshops, fitted with a Peugeot engine. The first International Cycle and Motorcycle Exhibition of 1910 featured the first production Morgan as a single-seater runabout. By 1911, HFS had produced his first two-seater, and the future of the Morgan car was determined. Three-wheelers, such as the Morgan, paid low road tax and low insurance

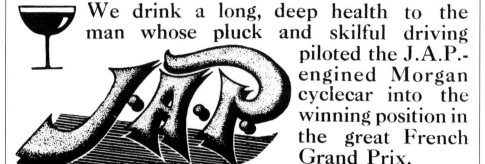
as they were classified as being of motorcycle origin, having no reverse, whereas four-wheeled cyclecars were recognised as cars. The car was constructed very lightly and was based on a tubular chassis held together by lugs and brazing in the manner of pedal and motor powered bicycles. The principal tube in the chassis ran from the front to the rear of the car. This tube had two transversely extending members at the front to which the JAP engine was fitted and on to which the front suspension (almost identical to that used on the Plus-8 to this day) was mounted. Independent front suspension by two vertical coil springs was a significant design feature. The main drive shaft ran through the tube to the bevel box at the rear. Here two dog clutches and two short chains (one for each of the two speeds – no reverse) comprised the transmission system. Braking was by means of two bands mounted on either side of the rear wheel, one of which was attached to the footbrake and the other to the handbrake. Steering was by means of a tiller, for the first few cars, which could conveniently be controlled from the single seat, and bodywork as such was almost non-existent, although the smart flat petrol tank at the front and the mudguards made for the appearance of a car with a forward bonnet, unlike the tricar concept.

The Morgan three-wheeler was first reviewed in *The Motor Cycle* in November 1910, just after it had appeared at the Olympia Exhibition. The reviewer begins by saying that the car should on no account be missed by visitors, and concludes by describing it as 'a very cleverly designed runabout for a single rider'. Herein lay one of the two major reasons for the lack of immediate success – people who liked the car held back from buying it, because they would not be able to take a passenger in it. The other reason for the somewhat slow launching of the car was the simple fact that it had not proved itself in trials and competitions, and this counted significantly in the early part of this century than it does now. Those who doubt this

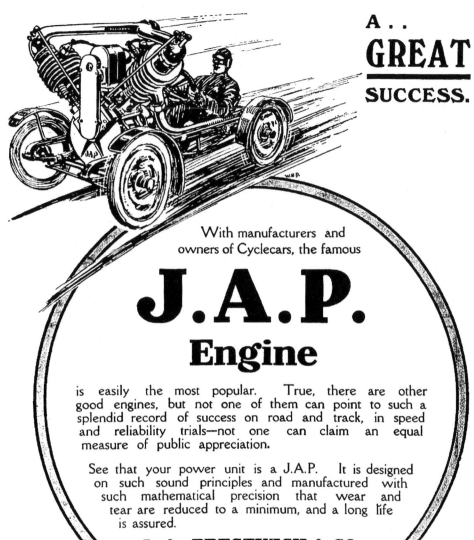

The JAP advertisement dated November 1912 which is of a ninety degree vee-twin, which disposition of the cylinders was produced exclusively for cyclecars and aeroplane engines. It has a remarkable similarity to the Precision engines of the same time.

McMinnies returns to the pits at Amiens in 1913 in his Morgan entered by the Cyclecar Club of Britain, knowing he has won the Cyclecar Grand Prix, but shortly he was to find that the French had organised the awards so that three-wheelers ran in a separate class and seemingly a different race. His mécanicien *was Frank Thomas, the secretary of the Cyclecar Club in Britain.*

H.F.S. Morgan and his wife Ruth at Stoke Lacey rectory in a 1915 De Luxe Morgan.

The front cover picture from a March 1918 Light Car and Cyclecar *of a Swiss-made MAG-engine in a Grand Prix model.*

should read the letter signed 'Enthusiast' in *The Motor Cycle* of November 1912, in which the writer says:

> *There are only three cyclecars the manufacturers of which have had the courage to compete in all or most of the yearly reliability trials, viz. The AC, the Morgan and the GWK. I venture to suggest that until the manufacturers of other cyclecars publicly demonstrate their quality, intending purchasers and especially the businessman, will not look at the results of their time and labour.*

HFS was not slow to tackle both these matters, and in the meantime, he was helped by Harrods taking on the first agency. The great Knightsbridge store was still an up-and-coming firm at this time and did not fail to notice any product with an interesting potential. Thus they were in touch with Mr Morgan soon after the show and made an agreement which benefited both sides. Other Morgan agencies soon followed.

The major boost achieved by a Morgan was to cover almost sixty miles in the hour at Brooklands in November 1912 driven by HFS in single-seater form, with a special ohv JAP engine. In the autumn of 1912, J.A. Prestwich Ltd offered their ninety-degree vee-twin with inlet over exhaust-valved engine for cyclecars and a number of manufacturers tried them. The specification was similar to the GN engine with the exception that it did not have a large external flywheel. HFS Morgan, having only just got into production, probably rejected the design, since he did not want to make any changes at that time. Years later the ninety-degree engine with ohv valve gear, was reconsidered by E.B. Ware and fitted in a

Morgan in May of 1923 for a trial at Brooklands. Val Page, who was JAP's designer at that time, said 'the trials showed excellent performance flexibility and reduced vibration…it could have been JAP's best ever, but times were unsettled…the project was delayed and finally abandoned.'

The first production Morgans had mounted a JAP side valve air-cooled V-twin motorcycle engine of 1,000cc at the front of a tubular chassis frame. Engines of 1,100cc were to follow later. There were two seats side-by-side and the design of the Morgan three-wheeler was set. A reasonable amount of power combined with light weight meant an excellent performance. The vehicle was safer than most three-wheelers, because the road-holding was above average. Three-wheelers, if fitted with soft suspension, have a tendency to roll on corners, which can cause digging in and the car turning over – a propensity only curable by making sure the suspension was rock hard.

The success of McMinnies in the Amiens event was lauded in Britain. HFS Morgan had also entered Morgans for the race – for himself with a JAP engine, and Rex Munday with a Green's Precision engine.

From this time, the Morgan three-wheeler was typecast as a sporting fast three-wheeler. This recipe made the Morgan popular with sportsmen, for whom the Grand Prix model, being based on the Amiens car, was produced in 1914: the first catalogued competition Morgan. Soon afterwards, an exiguous four-seater, the forerunner of the Family model of the 1920s, was listed.

After the First World War, Morgan continued to cater for all markets. Names changed, but the Standard model was the normal two-seater, also available in de Luxe form; the Family

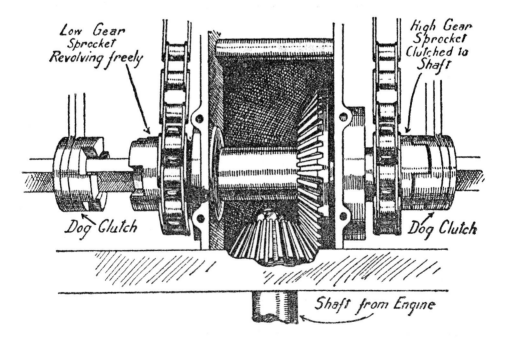

The two-speed Morgan used dog clutches keyed to the bevel shaft, that transmitted the power. The GN and Frazer Nash chain-drive transmission used the same principle of dog clutches.

WINNER OF TWO GOLD MEDALS
AND TWO SILVER MEDALS
in the Birmingham M.C.C. Passenger
Machine Trial, 12th April.
OTHER RECENT WINS—
Brooklands, 29th March, 100 Miles High Speed
Reliability Trial:—Class A, Mr. V. Busby, First.
Class B, Mr. A. W. Lambert, First;
        Mr. N. F. Holder, Second.

*Full
particulars
with
pleasure.*

MORGAN
MOTOR
CO., LTD.,
MALVERN.

model was the more capacious type, and the long-tailed Aero, later the Super Sports, was the Morgan intended for serious speed work. Engines were water or air-cooled to choice, most being supplied by JAP, or by Blackburne in the case of the competition models. The other great feature of the car was its remarkably high power-to-weight ratio of 90bhp per ton, which in effect immediately enabled the Morgan to be thought of as a sports car. In August 1919, an article appeared in *The Cyclecar* about a special four-seater Morgan that had been built for Mr E.B. Ware of the JAP engine company. Ware went on to be the racing hero of the Morgan enterprise competing directly with motor cars. The writing had been on the wall for a long time when Ware had a bad crash at Brooklands in 1924 and from thence forward the ACU, the organisation for motor cycles and sidecar outfits, was the competitive home for Morgan, whilst the RAC looked after cars. No longer in the same classes could Morgan compete against GN and the others, except in sprints such as those on Southport sands. In 1928 the New Cyclecar Club was formed to permit racing between light cars and Morgans at Brooklands.

By early October 1919, the new Morgan factory was fully operational and for the first time the firm had the capacity to build 2,500 cars per year, although shortage of engines kept the numbers down for the time being.

Morgan successes in France began again in 1919, the most notable being Paul Houel's victory in the Circuit de L'Eure on 16 August. This had a considerable impact on the sales of the French produced Morgan, which came out later in the year – the Darmont Morgan.

1922 was also the year in which Anzani-engined Morgans first began to make a name for themselves. In June, Harry Martin came first in the five-lap passenger handicap at Brooklands at 70.58mph and then second in a two-lap passenger handicap. British Anzani were not slow to advertise their Morgan successes.

When the Motor Cycle Show was held in November, the Morgan stand was a centre of attraction, and when Sir Harold Bowden took the Duke of York on a tour of the show he began by showing him the Morgans. Here the *pièce de résistance* was an Anzani-engined Aero Morgan with the body finished in nickel plate with black wings. The Duke, we are told, was much impressed by it, but perhaps this is understandable since he himself owned a Morgan-Anzani. Another reason for popular interest was that prices were again down – the Standard model cost only £128 and, like all the other models, was now offered for the first time with a Blackburne engine as an alternative to the JAP. The Family model was offered at £158 water-cooled or £148 air-cooled, and the Grand Prix at £155. The Anzani engine used in the Aero model was an ohv water-cooled unit with a water-heated induction pipe. The Morgan car company used to play off their engine suppliers against each other and the engine, which was most admired and fitted in the early 1920s was the vee-twin Anzani made by British Anzani. It was the Morgan endless drive to reduce the price for each unit that led to exhaust valves of lower quality being fitted and failing in service. This led to litigation and Archie Frazer-Nash (with Eric Burt of Mowlems) buying up the Anzani company from Charles Fox, a notable British pianoforte manufacturer. British Anzani – as British Anzani Engineering of Kingston on Thames – was reformed and supplied spare parts to individual Morgan owners, and later, after a meeting with HFS, engines to Morgans direct. The M3 Anzani engine was redesigned after the law suit with better cam design and valves, and were fitted to Morgans through the late 1920s and early 1930s.

Apart from the advent of Anzani and Blackburne engines, there was very little alteration in the Morgans at the Show. *Light Car and Cyclecar* of 30 March 1923 announced that front wheel brakes were available although a number of customers had already had this luxury fitted to their cars. Morgan had spent over two years perfecting the mechanism, but it had to be worked independently from the rear brakes by a hand lever. It was still considered that the extra stopping power should only be needed in an emergency.

1923 was also an historic year in that the total number of Morgans in circulation, including several hundred Darmont Morgans which had been made under licence in France, reached the 40,000 mark, so it was claimed. It is thought that a figure of 4,000 would be more accurate. HFS was obliged to extend his factory quite considerably that year to cope with the ever-increasing demand. The Pickersleigh Road factory was constantly being enlarged from the two shops built in the First World War, which were extended in 1919 with a special ceremony and again expanded in 1923 with yet another ceremony. A further extension was made in early 1930. The original garage was then sold.

The side-valve engines soldiered on for the basic 'Standard' models. Geared down steering to make the steering less startlingly direct was available in 1927. The Super Sports could attain 80mph in standard trim, while the less sporting types now had internal expanding front wheel brakes and electric starting.

In September 1928, Gwenda Stewart gained a number of world records in the 750cc three-wheeler class, driving a MEB three-wheeler. When these records were snatched away from her in November by H. Beart in his Morgan, she began to suspect that 'if you can't lick 'em – join 'em' was the best policy for her. Beart had raised Gwenda Stewart's hour record from 74.19 miles to 82.38 miles in one attempt, and this undoubtedly impressed her. Hereafter, she was to compete in a Morgan and was to be a most valuable asset to the Morgan cause.

When the Motor Cycle Show opened at Olympia in November 1928, it was revealed that only two makes of cyclecar were present: Morgan and Coventry-Victor. Both HFS and

Naylor & Root's South London showroom. (Photo courtesy of Mr Naylor)

Mr Weaver of Coventry-Victor lamented this, as they felt that a little more competition could only improve the three-wheeler cause. Visitors to the Morgan stand learned that a number of improvements had been made to the 1929 models. The bearings of the rear hub and bevel box were fitted with oil-retaining felt washers, and geared steering (which had been available on 1928 models at extra cost) now became standard. The dynamo drive was improved by the fitting of helical gears and the sliding axles on the front suspension were provided with a grease cavity.

The 1928 Show saw the passing of the Standard model, the cheapest two-seater machine now being the De Luxe. This had a new type of body on a long chassis and was priced, like the Family model, at £92. These non-sports models all had air-cooled side valve JAP engines of 980cc. Front wheel brakes were standard on all Morgans for 1929 except the cheapest De Luxe model, and electric starters could be fitted to any model for £8, although they needed some assistance on frosty mornings.

A De Luxe Morgan with an acetylene generator in front of the spare Castrol tin.

Morgan employed underage drivers for driving the cars around inside the works. The gear lever for the two-speed transmission is placed by the transverse bevel shaft, behind the driver.

The fastest car in the Morgan range was the Super Sports Aero, which cost £150. This car would hold its own as regards acceleration to about 60-70mph with most sports cars on the road. The Morgan's top speed, even without special tuning, was over 80mph. It certainly could run shoulder to shoulder with the chain drive Frazer Nash, which was in simple terms a development of the GN.

Morgan was losing customers to newer, more modern four wheel sports cars, such as the M-type MG. Improvements such as three speeds and reverse in a normal gearbox (though still with chain final drive) were available from 1931, and standard after 1932, and a modified 8hp Ford four-cylinder engine could be had from 1933, instead of a twin.

By 1933, the cheaper £100 Ford and Morris four-wheelers were the commercial problems with which to contend, and Morgan introduced detachable wheels just like a car. In 1935 the beginning of the end as a cyclecar manufacturer was detectable with the 8hp and 10hp Ford side-valve engines being offered side by side with a Matchless-engined vee-twin at the Motor Show. JAP having finally decided that they could not meet the Morgan lower pricing requirement. In 1936 the 4/4 Morgan four-wheeler was introduced and Morgan joined the car makers. After the Second World War Morgan completed a further twelve Matchless-powered vee-twins and went on producing the Ford powered units until 1952. Morgan, with the three-wheeler, had easily outlasted all its cyclecar competitors.

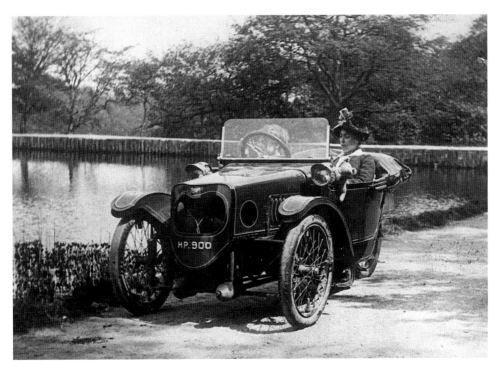

A 1920 De Luxe Morgan.

An Anzani-engined Grand Prix, driven by the Bournemouth agent for Morgan, Mr Primaveri, who is accompanied by his wife.

The Engine that Wins.

Skegness Speed Trials.

An amateur driver of a Morgan, fitted with a **9 h.p. British Anzani Engine**— describing his success at above speed trials— says: "In the 1100 c.c. Car event I **absolutely walked away with it** without any difficulty, and thereby **won a Silver Cup."**

Write for details :

The British ANZANI Engine Co., Ltd.,

30-32, Scrubbs Lane, Willesden, London, N.W. 10.

An Anzani advertisement of 1923.

H.F.S. Morgan and his wife Ruth in a Birmingham-Holyhead-Birmingham Trial of July 1924 driving a Blackburne-engined Aero Morgan.

George Goodall and Cecil Jay of Morgan as part of the 1925 Stock Machine Trial, run by the ACU (Auto Cyclists Union).

A 1931 Super Aero Morgan with an ohv JAP.

Dr Jake Alderson and the Revd Adrian Murray-Leslie competing with Jake's Matchless-powered Morgan in the 1983 MCC Edinburgh Trial.

4
The Carden and the AV Monocar

The Carden

The first Carden was designed by John Carden and built at his works, the Carden Engineering Co., at 83 East Street, Farnham, Surrey, early in 1913. It was of unusual design, even by cyclecar standards, and was a single-seater intended for racing. The car was driven by Carden himself in the first Sidecar and Cyclecar Race of $5\frac{3}{4}$ miles at the Brooklands Easter Monday meeting in 1913 when it started on the limit mark, but broke down on its second lap.

The car was streamlined for its day, the low build being made possible by putting the air-cooled 482cc single-cylinder JAP engine behind the back axle at the extreme rear end of the chassis. The seat was of hammock type and the highest point of the car was only inches above the road wheels. If the hammock seat gave way then the driver was in intimate contact with the road. It weighed a mere 2cwt and could lap Brooklands at 47mph.

Chain drive ran forward from the engine shaft to the back axle giving a 4:1 gear ratio. As there was no clutch, the driver push started and leapt in, which must have been somewhat hazardous with steering of the pivoted front axle type. It was claimed to be the same as a racing motorcyclist bump starting his bike, but the Carden was clearly a lot more hazardous, especially if the device had built up some speed.

The second Carden cyclecar built was immediately sold to Edward Tamplin who, in 1919, started to produce his own cyclecar, the Tamplin, the design of which was a copy of the Carden.

By April 1913, Carden production models were being offered, in similar form to the prototype racer, at £55, but the design included mudguards. The bodywork was of a wooden coffin shape made of $\frac{1}{2}$in pine with a weather-resistant top covering. The body was reinforced with steel cross members and a sheet steel scuttle with a pointed nose. The gear ratio was 5:1, so there can have been no gear box, but reference was made to a multi-disc clutch being incorporated in the roller chain drive to the back axle.

No mention was made of brakes, but it is probable that these were similar to those on the later production cars. These consisted of a belt rim on the back axle, alongside the sprocket, with two brake blocks, one operated by foot when the clutch lever was pressed to the limits of its movement and the other by hand lever.

The pivoted front axle had a coil spring sliding over a vertical strut fixed to the centre of the axle and, with the spring, sliding inside a tubular support on the frame. Double flexible cables, with ends adjustable for length, ran from the ends of the axle through copper guide tubes to a wooden drum under the steering wheel, which was mounted on a bracket fixed to the scuttle. Consideration was probably given to the use of a steering column with a bobbin at the lower end of it, but the space under the bonnet was so restricted that there would be no room after providing space for feet and pedals.

In May 1913, a department was formed to manufacture single-seaters of a quantity sufficient for sporting purposes; they could hardly have been described as suitable for touring.

They could now lap Brooklands at 51mph. In June, G.C. Holzapfel joined Carden in partnership in this project.

The list of cars that were to be manufactured in 1914 was given out in November 1913, but Carden used major motor manufacturer terms such as 'the programme' linked with 'announced'; there were three models known simply as the A, B and C. These were largely similar to the previous model except for the different engine options and the provision of starting handles. One of the joys of a single-seater Carden/AV Monocar is to observe the starting procedure as the driver stands behind the car and sets the throttle with one hand, whilst pulling on a toggle-shaped piece of wood attached to a chain drive to spin the engine over. Backfires were likely to feed the driver onto the top of the spark plugs. The wheelbase was 78in and the track 32in and the frame and body were still of wood.

There was a direct chain drive with an Albion multi-disc clutch so, in the absence of a gear box, to achieve a lower gear ratio to get away from the start was achieved by slipping the clutch. This arrangement probably prompted the fitting of a shock-absorbing device in the axle sprocket. Brakes were as before. There being no separate frame, the rear quarter elliptic springs were attached to the wooden body unit.

The A engine was an air-cooled single-cylinder JAP of 85mm x 85mm (483cc); the B was a twin of 70mm x 85mm (654cc); and the C was also a twin of 70mm x 65mm (496cc). The C model drove by chain from the clutch to a two-speed box on a countershaft and then by chain to the axle. Otherwise, the B and C were similar to the A. The weight of the C was close to 310lb and the prices of the A, B and C were £59 10s, £67 and £72 10s respectively.

Demand was evidently good as, in February 1914, the firm – now a limited company – moved from Farnham to larger premises in Somerset Road, Teddington. In May, John Carden and his co-director Holzapfel took records in the 750cc cyclecar class at Brooklands at 61.12mph for the kilometre, 59.91mph for the mile and 55.75mph for ten miles, using a 590cc JAP single-cylinder engine. This performance gained a number of column inches in

A klaxon horn would have been an extra for the Carden.

the Press. The 1915 models, brought out at the 1914 Show, were still monocars, but now with modified rear suspension and transmission. The A model was evidently being dropped, but the B and C were continued with twin-cylinder JAP engines of 647cc and 496cc. The rear suspension kept the quarter elliptics attached to the body, with radius arms running back from the axle to the extremities of the frame, which acted as the engine bearer. The transmission of the B was, as before, a direct chain drive but that of the C was a quite remarkable two-speed arrangement. This continued the use of the large sprocket on the axle and the small sprocket and clutch on the engine shaft and these, when connected, gave high gear.

Low gear was engaged by pressing the gear pedal, which withdrew the clutch and raised a friction wheel from its idling position to engage with another friction wheel on the engine shaft. The clutch, having been disengaged, allowed the sprocket to revolve freely on the engine shaft. A sprocket was fixed to, and therefore revolved with, the friction wheel and when these were raised to the low gear position and the friction wheels came into engagement, the sprocket was engaged at the same time, as their counterparts on the engine shaft. These differences in diameter provided the low gear ratio of $8\frac{1}{2}$:1 and the high of $4\frac{3}{4}$:1.

Specification.

8 h.p. Twin Engine, air-cooled. 3-Speeds. 60 M.P.G. Seat Starter. Extreme accessibility. Ample power. Weight, 3½ cwt. only. Windscreens and hoods now available

CARDEN

Monocars—and—Two Seaters

are the result of nine years' experience in the design and manufacture of the ultra-light four-wheeler.

P R O M P T   D E L I V E R Y

The Times

10th Sept., 1919, writing of the General Efficiency Trial held recently by the Junior Car Club, says:—

"Two types were represented—the CARDEN and the ———. In design they are quite different, but they are really closely connected by the fact that both were originally designed by the same man, Mr. CARDEN, who was, one believes, the first to produce and place upon the market a practical single-seater four-wheeler embodying much of the comfort of the touring car with the lightness and constructional economy of the motor-cycle. . . . . The several Carden competitors behaved admirably. They were exceedingly fast, and demonstrated their ability to be brought to rest and smoothly restarted on a 1 in 8 gradient. In this respect they were clearly much better than many of the four-cylinder light cars. . . . . . There was no question as to the Carden's pace. . . . . . The brakes appeared to be able to pull the Carden up with extraordinary rapidity."

N O   D I S A P P O I N T M E N T

Place your Order NOW with the firm with experience.

The Carden Engineering Co., Ascot

Lamps were fitted to the front mudguards, together with a dynamo. Tools were provided on the 'de luxe' model, for £85, the standard version being priced at £73 10s.

For the spring of 1915, a two-seater was marketed. Basically, it was as the C model, but with a staggered passenger seat on the driver's right due to the controls being placed at the driver's left hand. A neat engine cover hinged backwards for access to the engine; it had holes through which the air-cooled cylinders protruded when it was closed. In November 1915 dimensional alterations were made, these being wheelbase 74in, track 30in and overall width 38in. Like many small car companies, the Carden Co. ceased car production, as the facilities were required to produce components for the war. Larger companies produced vehicles that the armed forces required and hence were in a good position to start up civil production when the war was over.

Carden obviously served his country in the First World War since afterwards he was referred to in the press as Capt. Carden. The post-war model was announced in December 1918. It had the same 654cc JAP engine with the multi-disc clutch but the engine was fitted with an extra oil reservoir. The two-speed chain drives were operated by dog clutches, which was an improvement on the movable friction wheels of 1914. Direct steering was used with a fixed front axle the hub assemblies of which were located between vertical helical springs on sliding pillars.

In February 1919 a new Carden two-seater appeared, resembling the monocar but with the large 85mm x 85mm (964cc) JAP engine. It was evidently a stop-gap until Carden could announce his redesigned car in April, when his company had moved to Kennel Ride, Ascot.

During the War, the company was sold and there is a strong possibility that Capt. Carden did not tell the new owners that he proposed to carry on manufacturing under his original name. An argument between Carden and the purchasers, Ward & Avery, arose. In 1915 Carden stated that he had ceased to manufacture cars and the new owners would make the Carden under the name of AV. AV was located in the works at Teddington, previously occupied by Carden Engineering. During the War, these works were modernised and AV car production began in 1918.

Capt. Carden restarted his cyclecar venture in 1919 under the name of Carden, but Ward & Avery disputed his right to do this on the grounds that he had sold all the Carden assets, including the name of the cyclecar, when he disposed of the Carden Engineering Co. assets in 1915. Carden claimed that he had only sold the cyclecar parts and not the name, but his new cyclecar was not of the monocar type, now being made by Ward & Avery. The difficulty was settled in a way which was never explained, but which enabled Capt. Carden to market his new type of monocoque cyclecar.

The new Carden, with few modifications, was sold as the Tamplin. The new model appeared in April 1919, and was a simple car with the passenger staggered behind as before. The mudguards being straight planks from front to back at bonnet level and with flat side panels for the body made of a composition material which was lighter than wood. As competitors unsympathetically stated, they were 'made of cardboard'. The engine was an air-cooled JAP or Blackburne at the front of the car, which was a major design change. A chain drive ran to the gearbox, mounted amidships, from whence a single belt drove the near side rear wheel. The clutch was operated by a pedal, which applied a brake to the gearbox belt pulley on full depression. A hand lever applied a block brake to the rear belt rim. The suspension was unchanged, with rear quarter elliptics and coils at the front. It was a single-seater and a 'super sporting two-seater' was offered.

In December 1919 the two-seater, the 'new' Carden was available. It was a much wider car and driver and passenger could sit side by side in a conventional mode. It should have been important in the history of motoring, for it was the first post-war £100 car. It was fitted with a flat twin two-stroke engine of Carden manufacture built into the back axle.

The AV Monocar

The design of the AV, the first of which appeared in late 1918, was very similar to the earlier single-seater Cardens, particularly as to the streamlined type of body and the rear mounting of the engine which was a water-cooled V-twin JAP of 85mm x 85mm (961cc) with water pump and multi-disc clutch. The transmission was a redesigned version of the Carden. A chain drive ran from the engine to a large chain wheel on the back axle and locked to it by a dog clutch for high gear. Low gear and reverse were obtained by enclosed spur gears engaged by dog clutches.

The track at the front was 40in and at the rear 32in, the makers claiming that the wider front track was to improve appearance and avoid an inswept frame which, with a pivoted front axle, would have been necessary to give a good steering lock. It was likely, though, that the lack of a differential influenced the decision to have a narrow rear track

A large belt wheel was fixed close to the chain wheel and two brake blocks provided foot and hand operated brakes. The steering was of Carden type, with wire cables running through guide tubes from the front axle to a drum under the scuttle-mounted steering wheel.

A toolbox with a padlock would have been an extra for this Tamplin.

Modifications appeared in August 1919, chiefly to the power train. An epicyclic two-speed gear ($4\frac{1}{4}$ and 8:1) was fitted to the engine shaft and drove the back axle which had a large chain wheel with shock absorbing hub. A clutch was worked by a hand lever and the left pedal on the floor, where 'neutral' was central and 'high' was out.

The engines available were V-twin air-cooled JAPs, one of 70mm x 85mm (654cc) and the other of 85mm x 85mm (961cc). A two-seater was also advertised with screen, tools, horn and disc wheels and a water cooled 961cc JAP engine but this did not appear in the market place and in May 1920 it was stated that its production had had to be postponed 'because of supply difficulties'. The prices of the monocars were £135 for the model with the larger engine and £130 for the smaller, and neither had any equipment such as windscreen or hood.

It is possible, however, that a redesign exercise for a two-seater caused second thoughts about production of the prototype two-seater as at the same time, in May 1920, it was announced that a new two-seater, the Bicar, was being developed from the monocar. This had the 961cc JAP air-cooled engine which, being partially enclosed, had a fan and air ducting in front of it. The epicyclic gears were replaced by a sliding gearbox and multi-disc clutch with chain drive to the axle. Brakes were of drum and contracting band type.

The centrally-pivoted front axle was retained, with the addition of a single quarter elliptic spring-mounted on the front of the wooden frame. The front end of the main leaf rested on a pad on the front axle below the spiral spring where it was able to slide, thus giving a better ride than would be possible with a spiral spring only.

The body was slightly wider and longer than that of the monocar, so as to accommodate the bench type seat behind the driver for the passenger, who could sit with legs extended beside the driving seat, there being a space between this and the near side of the body. This was really no change at all, but a slight increase in the dimensions did provide greater comfort.

The monocars were continued with their engine options, epicyclic gears and front suspension with the central quarter elliptic spring. The rear suspension was by quarter elliptics fixed to the frame and with their rear ends sliding on pads on the axle mountings. The axle therefore required locating, which was done by beautifully engineered radius rods running to the ends of the frame under the engine mounting.

The 1921 programme, announced at the 1920 Motor Show in October, continued with both Bicar and Monocars, the Bicar reverting to epicyclic gears with alternative ratios of $4\frac{1}{2}$ top gear and alternative bottom gears of 9:1 and 11:1. The gear ratios on the Monocars varied with the engine sizes, being $5\frac{1}{4}$:1 and close to 16:1 for the 70mm x 85mm 654cc. Higher final drive gears were available for the 772cc and 961cc variants. Suspension and steering were unchanged.

By show time in October 1921, it had been decided that the Bicar needed updating and both Bicar and Monocars went over to fixed front axles, quarter elliptic springs and Ackermann steering. The Bicar used the same JAP engine with its oil tank in the scuttle and coupled either to a Juckes epicyclic gear of $4\frac{1}{2}$:1 and $11\frac{1}{2}$:1 or a Sturmey Archer three-speed box of $4\frac{1}{2}$:1, $7\frac{1}{3}$:1 and 12:1. Reverse was now supplied on all models, as the increasing weight of the design made it necessary. The side-by-side seats on the Bicar resulted in the wheelbase being shortened by a foot. The price, excluding lighting, was £155.

The Monocar was now offered in only one version with the 961cc JAP, but the Bicar range was added to by a sports two-seater, without equipment, with an air-cooled Blackburne engine and three-speed Sturmey Archer box, plus a four-seater Runabout, the rear seat being suitable for children only, and a two-seater runabout with epicyclic gears.

Although a two-seater with Blackburne engine was still being offered in 1922 it must have been evident that the end was in sight. The company's formal end came in 1926.

The old and new squires inspect the AV Monocar.

A 1912 Bédélia and a 1918 AV Monocar belonging to Mike Bullett and photographed by fellow Bédélia owner Mike Kimball.

5

The Bédélia and the Cyclecar in France

In France in 1910, there was an urgent need for a low cost motorcycle-based motor car, as there were rumblings around the world of a petroleum price war, leading to possible stronger actions. The USA was over-burdened with cheap petrol – with some states having petrol more readily available and cheaper than good clean water. Petrol came to France from Java and Romania and the price was rapidly increasing. The French government had instituted research into the production of benzole and drilling for oil in the various parts of the French Empire, but in 1910, oil had yet to be discovered in the French dominions.

The cyclecar movement was extremely lucky to find a whole host of active motoring journalists to promote 'the new motoring'. In the autumn of 1910, W.G. McMinnies was in Paris, to cover the Paris Motor Show, although as it was reported, there are always excellent reasons for a journalist being in Paris. He was at that time on the staff of *The Motor* and was seated at a boulevard café table when, above the rumble of the traffic, he heard the crisp bark of a twin-cylinder engine. He leapt to his feet. Trundling happily past his astonished eyes was a vehicle the like of which he had never seen. A wooden coffin, unpainted, running on four motorcycle wire wheels, the top open and containing a man in front behind an engine and another, tandem fashion, with a steering wheel at the back.

McMinnies took instant action and tore down the street in pursuit of the crackling apparition until, almost out of breath he saw the vehicle held in a traffic jam and grabbed his chance. The startled Frenchman gazed at the incoherent Englishman for a moment and then, with a grin, pulled over to the kerb. Robert Bourbeau was big, blond and bearded. McMinnies had the first close-up of the Bédélia and, from that moment, he was a convert, blazing with all the zeal of those who have just seen the light. A vee-twin engine of 1,056cc provided 9bhp at 2,400rpm by chain to a countershaft midway along the chassis, from whence belts on each side drove the rear wheels. There was no clutch, no gearbox, and reverse motion was produced by getting out and pushing backwards. However, to keep the engine running in traffic, the back axle could be moved forward, allowing the belts to run slack. The driving pulleys were in duplicate, one larger than the other, to provide two forward speeds. To change 'gear' was a simple operation, once it was mastered, of letting go of the steering wheel, grabbing a stick (provided) in each hand and, sticking them under the belts, yanking them over onto the other pulley in one quick, neat motion that must have been pretty to watch. A somewhat slower change, but one that allowed the machine to be steered in the meantime, could be carried out by utilising the sticks one at a time, a method much preferred by the passenger in front, unless he offered to do the job himself. Steering was almost equally simple and effective, for the straight, tubular front axle was swivelled about its centre by means of wires which, at the business end, wound round a bobbin.

Lost in admiration, McMinnies stood oblivious of the hurrying crowds staring at him, gazing down the tree-lined boulevard as the Bédélia clattered on its way in and out of the traffic and vanished from sight in a cloud of blue smoke and the fumes of hot oil. The die

A Bédélia with a sophisticated windscreen for the forward placed passenger. The photograph is believed to have come from Rhodesia.

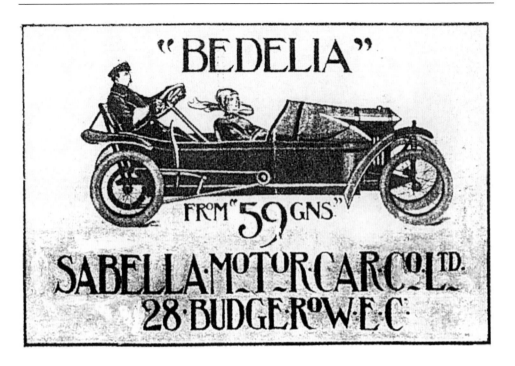

was cast. A new form of motoring was born. McMinnies wrote up his story in the 8 September 1910 issue of *The Motor Cycle* which must have been the first ever words published in Britain on 'The New Motoring' under the heading of 'A Novel Quadricycle':

Reference had been made in a daily newspaper to a French motor 'car' which has made its appearance in Paris and is to be sold at a hitherto unheard-of price. Investigation has revealed the fact that this vehicle is in reality a quadricycle, the passengers being carried tandem fashion. It possesses so many interesting features that we know a description and illustrations of it will interest all motor-cyclists who contemplate taking a passenger with them on their rides. We have, therefore, induced the makers, Bourbeau and Devaux, to provide us with the salient points of this somewhat ingenious little 'véhicule à deux'.

No excuse is needed for describing in a journal devoted to motor cycles the Bédélia four-wheeler, as this novel quadricycle has been named, because the French licensing authorities have accepted it as a motor cycle. The builders are also prepared to fit pedals, to be used for starting the motor only, or not to be used at all, and with this innocent equipment the French owner can continue to enjoy a car while paying the modest taxation of a motor cycle. In a country holding the record for high motor car taxation, this is an advantage not to be despised.

The Bédélia is a low-built quadricycle, carrying its passengers tandem fashion, the driver being at the rear, and his companion occupying the centre of the long boat-like body in a very reclining position. Obviously, to be marketed at £48 to £68, the vehicle must be remarkably simple in construction.

Between two tubular axles, 8ft 3in distant one from the other, is a long low body forming the frame. The main members are armoured wood, with the sides covered with sheet aluminium. The front portion is abruptly narrowed to the smallest width possible for mounting the motor, which on the two cheaper models is a single-cylinder air-cooled Quentin of 3½ or 4½ hp. On a larger model a two-cylinder vee-motor is employed, also air-cooled.

The motor is enclosed at each side by sliding sheet metal panels, the front being left open in order to allow a free draught of air. Thus, while being thoroughly protected against mud splashing, the motor receives as strong an air current as it would on a motor bicycle. There is very little about the engine that calls for attention, unless it be the arrangement for tightening the belt. This is performed by slightly slackening off the bolts holding the motor lugs to the frame and gently driving in a wooden wedge, kept permanently in position between the rear of the crank case and a transverse member. This allows the engine to be moved forward without destroying the alignment. Ignition is by storage battery and coil, although provision is now being made for fitting a magneto on the two-cylinder model. The carburettor is a well-known make, and lubrication is by means of a pump. As on a motor bicycle, the petrol tank is mounted directly above the engine, and forms the top of the frontless bonnet. The tank is of steel, with electro-acetylene welded joints, making leakages impossible.

A single chain takes the drive from the engine to a counter-shaft placed across the centre of the frame. A band brake is fitted on this shaft, and is operated by a pedal, which also lifts the exhaust valve; thus the first touch of the pedal raises the exhaust valve, and a further applica-tion applies the brake. From the counter-shaft the drive is taken to the rear wheels by means of two belts, one on each side. There is neither gear box nor differential, the latter having been found unnecessary with this combination of long wheelbase, narrow track, and belt drive. A simple method of lowering the gear ratio, however, is provided. On each extremity of the counter-shaft are mounted two pulleys of different diameters. If a steep hill has to be climbed, if the roads are heavy, or if a large amount of luggage has to be carried, the belts are slipped off the large pulleys and on to the smaller ones. The change is made possible by the rear axle having a fore and aft motion, and it is this fore and aft motion which fulfils the function of a clutch. The springs are inverted semi-elliptics, shackled at their forward ends to the frame member, attached to a pivoting hanger in the centre, and at the rear linked to the tubular axle. The shifting of the axle is obtained by means of a lever on the right hand side; about half a

The long wheelbase of the Bédélia is self-evident.

AUTOMOBILETTES

A. COIGNET & J. DUCRUZEL

The Automobilette 'all of the Camel', expressing the long distances the Automobilette could go without refuelling, that is 'sober or temperate' in its habits

A French Automobilette which was an uprated and more sophisticated Bédélia. It was advertised in Britain at the end of 1912 from £104 as a 'sporty runabout' and 'a good business machine'.

dozen notches are provided on the quadrant corresponding to different positions of the axle. Advantage is taken of the second pulley on the counter-shaft to start the engine. A length of belt is wrapped round the outer pulley and with a touch on the valve lifter pedal to release the compression the engine is spun round.

The Bédélia was manufactured by Messrs Borbeau & Devaux, with Devaux initially funding construction, and was so named because of a popular song of 1910 called Bédélia. It also fitted in with the B and D initials of the founders. The victory that the French said the Bédélia had in winning the 1913 Cyclecar Grand Prix was a fillip to the concept of cyclecars in France and an even bigger incentive to Morgan in Britain as the two nations savoured the victories of the two different cars in the same event: 'Everyone has won and all shall have prizes', as it was said in *Alice in Wonderland*.

All over the world the tandem seating of the Bédélia was copied. The Noël, like the Bédélia, was offered in single-seater or tandem form. The Automobilette closely followed the Bédélia in design. The first models were steered from the rear and a monocar version was also offered. The steering was later moved to the front compartment. The car was made in Billancourt in Paris and by 1914 was moving to becoming a light car with a four-cylinder engine.

The other French cyclecar manufacturers were impressed by the speed and road holding of the McMinnies Morgan at the 1913 Cyclecar Grand Prix, even if the awards did not reflect the Morgan 'victory'. Immediately following the race, Darmont, Franquebalm and Baudeloque spoke with HFS. Imports of Morgans followed with 150 sold in the year, but the War brought an end to this connection for the time being.

W.D. Hawkes in the Dew, Violet in the Violet-Bogey and Archie Nash in the GN are all on the grid at Amiens in 1913.

Post-First World War

After the War, the Bédélia company was sold and the new model did not come until 1921 and probably in prototype form only and was never a success.

Darmont took out a distributing licence from Morgan and Paul Houel won the Cyclecar class at the Circuit de L'Eure on 16 August 1919, which was a major stimulus to sales of the Morgan. The 1919 Darmont-produced cars were Morgans with MAG engines from Geneva, but they had subtleties in the body shape which suggest that the bodies were French-made. Darmont, as importer of components, would not have had to pay the full car import duty. In late 1921, Darmont moved from a distributor's agreement to a manufacturing licence. The car was not called a Darmont-Morgan, but solely a Morgan, built under licence by R. Darmont and later 'French Licence – R. Darmont'. Darmont used every opportunity to race his cars. It is said that HFS had acquired an eight-valve MAG engine for use in the prospective 1914 Amiens Grand Prix. He sold this engine to Darmont and it was used for record attempts in France and was regularly loaned to Darmont distributors to race, throughout the 1920s. Darmont employed works drivers for competitive events. His brother and business partner, André, raced for Darmont as well.

The Darmont range of cars followed the Malvern-made cars, but he made his own versions of the JAP side valve twin, in air-cooled and water-cooled form, the crankcases being embossed 'The Morgan Runabout'. He also produced a light van – the Camionette. In 1925 he produced the 'Morgan – modèle Darmont Special' with his own version of the Blackburne twin. At this time the grand sounding Etoile de France model was also introduced. In 1931 he fitted the Morgan three-speed gearbox to the Special. In 1935 the Aerolux model had a side valve twin, fitted with the three-speed gearbox together with a front similar to the Morgan F type. In 1936 the four-wheeled 'V Junior' with a water-cooled side valve twin appeared. Throughout his life he maintained a good relationship with HFS and made regular visits for purchase of components to Malvern and to discuss developments. In 1939 being of the Jewish faith he fled France to Spain. When the factory was handed back to him in 1946 he decided not to resume manufacture.

A 1914 Violet-Bogey with a two-cylinder water-cooled engine and friction disc drive and a final chain.

Violet driving the Violet-Bogey with a four-cylinder engine of 1100cc with friction drive and final drive by chain in the AC de l'Ouest race of 1913.

It is surmised that the first 100 GNs built in France by Salmson were sold through Gaston, Wigmore & Williams to the Paris police.

Stuart Sandford, born in Britain, spent almost all his life in France. In the early 1920s he started to sell his version of the Morgan three-wheeler in Paris, while Darmont was assembling his Morgan in Courbevoie. Sandford had bought a Darmont and competed with it. He was a good friend of HFS Morgan. He raced Morgans throughout 1919-1921 and was a salesman for Darmont. He decided to make a three-wheeler of his own, but of a higher quality than the Darmont. He built a prototype in 1921 using a four-cylinder Ruby engine of 1,100cc and remained faithful to that engine for the rest of the car's life. The Sandford, other than retaining Morgan-type front suspension and three wheels rapidly moved away from the cyclecar style of construction and became a light car.

The end of the sports cyclecar in France can be attributed to the Cyclecar Grand Prix of 1921, which was run at Le Mans that September. The race was of four hours' duration and Lombard in the new Salmson, which had a four-cylinder engine and conventional transmission, won at an average speed of 55mph. The car had a GN type, tubular, brakeless front axle, but in all other respects the car was a new design. Monsieur Violet was second in a Mourre, who had won the previous year's race in the same car, but then named a Major; Chabreiron was third in an EHP with Sabipa on a Weler fourth, and fifth a long way behind was a Morgan.

It was fortunate that an agreement was made in 1919 between GN and Salmson for Salmsons to make the GN, for in May 1920 the French government prohibited the import of motor vehicles. The whole of the European car industry was living in fear of a flood of American cars on the market.

The places which imported the GN and later Salmson were New York, Argentina, Madagascar, Algeria, Morocco, Vietnam, Belgium, Switzerland and Spain; and when the four-cylinder Salmsons came on the market the list of countries expanded to include the West Indies, Australia, Czechoslovakia, Austria, Greece and New Zealand.

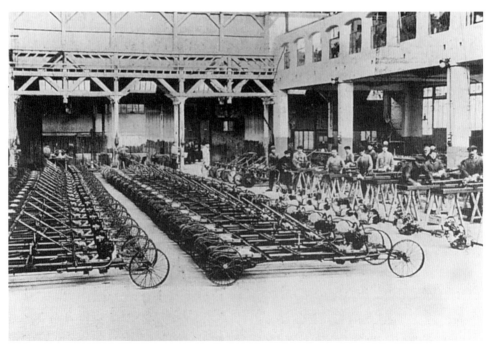

The Salmson factory at Billancourt with at least sixty complete GN chassis.

Salmsons and their agents were active in overseas markets and this is a French built GN in Egypt.

André Lombard (later to be a works driver for Salmson) worked for Gaston, Williams & Wigmore, Anglo-French car dealers who bought cars in one country and sold in the other. This firm were agents for Chapuis Dornier, together with Sigma, who manufactured cars using Ballot, SCAP and CIME engines. Lombard went to work for Salmson to set up their GN production line. The first 100 cars were supplied by Salmson to Gaston, Williams & Wigmore in Paris, for them to sell, notably to the Paris police. Salmson as an aeroplane engine manufacturer had little knowledge of the nuances of selling motor cars. Ron Godfrey and Archie Nash were aware of the potential production of the French factory, when they were surprised to find on a visit to the 1919 Paris Salon, about half a dozen of the French-built GNs running around, only three months after Salmson had received the drawings. Salmson managed to get properly jigged volume production underway from scratch in ten months. André Lombard became a key figure in the car manufacturing side of Salmsons. He was responsible for the introduction of the four-cylinder Salmson type AL (doubtless standing for his name) in 1921 for the Swiss Six Days Trial. The car was built to a conventional car design with little of the cyclecar in its construction. It did have a GN-type tubular front axle, but fitted with tubular radius rods. The rear axle brake drums also appear to be GN in origin. Lombard departed in 1923, eventually to market his own cars, and perhaps it is fitting that the last recorded GN sale by Salmson was of chassis No.1563, and that it should have been to Lombard on 21 May 1924.

The French Engines

French automobile manufacturers were legion. Many of these constructors had to rely on subcontractors for engines, rear axles, front ends and even complete chassis. Many a proud new French automobile owed its existence to these enterprising subcontractors in the 1900-

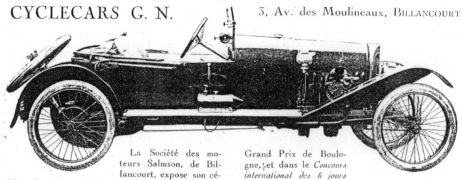

Société des Moteurs SALMSON

CYCLECARS G. N.　　　　　　3, Av. des Moulineaux, Billancourt

La Société des moteurs Salmson, de Billancourt, expose son célèbre Cyclecar G. N., type A. F., modèle 1922.

Le Cyclecar G. N. a été le véritable champion de France tourisme en 1921. On lui a décerné la médaille d'or dans le *Concours d'endurance*, la médaille d'or dans *Paris-Pyrénées-Paris*, la médaille d'or dans le *Critérium des Anciens Motocyclistes militaires*.

Dans le *Meeting de Boulogne*, le Cyclecar G. N. a remporté tout à la fois la Coupe Pickett et le Grand Prix de Boulogne, et dans le *Concours international des 6 jours* en Suisse, il s'est vu décerner la grande médaille d'or et la Coupe du Président de la République.

Le moteur du Cyclecar G. N., est à deux cylindres en V à ailettes (84 × 98). Il est à trois vitesses et comporte une marche arrière.

Tous les amateurs auront plaisir de retrouver le Cyclecar G. N. au Salon de l'Automobile dans la Grande Nef au Stand 64.

The Salmson, a period advertisement.

1925 period. GN in England in 1922 sought help in obtaining forgings and castings from France. Charles Lewington, who was GN's parts and service manager in 1923, said that the four-cylinder engine fitted to the shaft-drive car came via Gregoire. The GN sales pamphlet shows this water-cooled engine as 1,098cc (62mm x 91mm) and a photograph shows the most distinguishing feature to be a hinged rocker box cover to expose the push-rod side of the valve gear.

The belief that GN used the 'cheaper Chapuis-Dornier engine, rather than the DFP', was based on an interview with Ron Godfrey and he had left GN when the final 'production' car was ready. GN's catalogue description of the engine does not fit the Chapuis-Dornier, which was 1,095cc (59mm x 100mm). It was used by literally hundreds of small manufacturers in the early 1920s, without any reliability problems or 'endless troubles and the guarantee claims [that] finally completely bankrupted the company,' which was the comment that Ron Godfrey had made regarding the engines. DFP had started to make their own engines in 1912, the 1,100cc engine of the car they called the DF Petite was bought in from CIME. Gregoire also made engines for their cars in Paris before the war, but in 1920 they arranged for Hinstin in Maubeurge to make a light car for them using the same 1,099cc CIME engine (62mm x 91mm). It resembles exactly the picture of the engine in the shaft-drive GN sales leaflet.

The engine was made by Compagnie Industrielle de Moteurs à Explosions, CIME, whose factory was at Fraisse near St Etienne. They made a whole range of engines for car manufacturers, with the 1,099cc four-cylinder engine of 62mm bore and 91mm stroke, which CIME listed giving 20bhp at 3,000rpm with a compression ratio of 5:1. The block and crankcase were cast in one piece in iron, and the cylinder head had the carburettor on the nearside and the exhaust on the offside; it was unusual in 1920 for a proprietary engine of this sort to have a cross-flow cylinder head. The camshaft, magneto, dynamo and oil pump were driven by a train of gears at the front of the engine. The camshaft operated overhead valves by pushrods, which were external to the block and only covered by a simple aluminium plate, and via rockers, which were covered by a valve cover. This valve cover was hinged, as seen from the illustrations in the *Light Car & Cyclecar*, but this appears to be merely a bit of artist's licence, as such an arrangement would have interfered with the exhaust manifold.

The crankshaft with two main bearings fed oil under pressure from a pump, and the cooling was by thermo-syphon. This engine had a reputation for overheating. GNs were not the only people to suffer overheating, and one can assume that customers demanded a solution to these problems. Sometime in 1923, CIME produced a second series of this engine of the same bore and stroke which had a CIME plate riveted to the crankcase. The blocks are much longer and wider with greater cylinder spacings to increase the water jacket capacity, and the push-rods are enclosed.

Hinstin made a cyclecar for Gregoire which used the CIME engine and which had a transverse leaf spring at the front. The 1923 shaft-drive GN chassis and components did not necessarily come from Hinstin, but it appears to be probable.

The French nation seemed to be interested in the bizarre in all aspects of cyclecar design even as late as 1924 when, to a disinterested observer, it was all over. Monsieur Leroy built a three cylinder, two-stroke, water-cooled engine with a further three cylinders beneath the firing cylinders which were pumping cylinders; Monsieur Violet competed with the Leroy-Violet in 1927. He also built several cars with his name featured with Major, Mourre, Huascar, Galba and Leroy. The most important was the Sima-Violet which sported a flat, horizontally disposed Sima two-stroke of 500cc.

The Lafitte was built up to 1928 and featured a three-cylinder radial engine, which was pivoted by a cockpit lever so that the flywheel presented different tracks to the friction transmission, giving four nominal forward speeds and an optional four in reverse. It was imported into England at £100.

Archie Frazer-Nash used the Ruby engine for the Frazer Nash GNs assembled in Kingston upon Thames. The Ruby engine was fitted to many cars, such as the D'Yrsan of Asnières, which had moved further away from the Morgan style of three-wheeler to use a gearbox and shaft drive, from the moment the cars were first produced in the early 1920s.

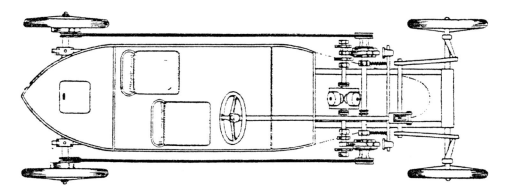

The post-First World War Bédélia transmission system had fixed axles and the three forward speeds and reverse gearing was obtained by friction discs running edge to edge.

A French Darmont-built Morgan for the 1921 Grand Prix at Le Mans.

'Sabipa', actual name Louis Charavel, in his entry of a Weler, fitted with a two stroke twin cylinder Violet engine at the 1921 Coupe des Voiturettes, Le Mans.

Mrs Sydney Cummings, mother of Ivy Cummings, driving a Ronteix, which was sold in Britain as a Commicar. The French-built Ronteix was more of a light car than a cyclecar, but its final transmission was by chain.

Charles Chapuis and Charles Dornier were both natives of Besançon, in eastern France. They began working together in 1904, when Dornier was thirty. They set up their company, Chapuis-Dornier, in January 1905. The factory was at the Quai de Strasbourg, in Besançon. Their aim was not to manufacture vehicles and they planned to specialise in the manufacture of proprietary 'off the shelf' engines for the variety of cars from cyclecars to the middle range, that were being built by a multitude of small manufacturers throughout France. They were not unique, for the French builders of cars had the choice of SCAP, CIME, Ruby and other engines, not necessarily made in France.

Chapuis-Dornier unveiled their first four-cylinder engine, a 65mm x 120mm design with a capacity of 1,592cc. The crankcase was made in three sections and the centre main bearing was supported by the central section. To this, the two side sections of the crankcase were bolted. It was claimed not only to be very rigid, but also inexpensive to manufacture. The engines were a great success, both in France and abroad. More than 2,000 were sold during 1910 alone. From 1912, the firm was renamed Dornier et Cadet, constructeurs. Charles Chapuis had now departed. He had sold his shares in the company to Louis Cadet, a Parisian.

The French government had engineered this trend by offering tax incentives to small engines. A new small engine, the 162lb CY4, was aimed specifically at this cyclecar market. The CY4 delivered 13hp at 1,900rpm and could reach 2,000rpm. It was offered with a three-speed gearbox.

Chapuis-Dornier also designed an 1,100cc capacity 79.5mm x 110mm V-twin engine. Fed by a 26mm carburettor, it gave 15.7hp at 2,000rpm with a compression ratio of $4\frac{1}{2}$:1. This

André Lombard at the wheel of the 1921 AL Salmson. This car was the first Salmson of their design.

engine was probably commissioned specifically by Janemian for the cyclecar he manufactured in the 1920s. The complete design for the cyclecar was the work of Sigmund Gerster. It seems unlikely that this V-twin engine was sold to many other builders.

In 1919 the company had a new agent in London – A. Picard of 4 New Burlington Street, London W1. But the market in Britain for the kind of engine that Chapuis-Dornier made had shrunk considerably since the war.

Post-1945, the cyclecar was not dead in France, for Monsieur Goudard assembled a number of studies of pedal-powered devices that could be up-rated with an engine. This was published as a do-it-yourself book by SIA in France. There was a resurgence in the demand for cyclecars or microcars as they tended to be called and a number of firms flourished for a short time. Charles Mochet of Puteaux, near Paris, built bicycles and his first cyclecar of the 1920s was powered by pedal cycle. In 1951 Charles Mochet's production plant in Puteaux started production on a new model, the CM-125 fitted with the correct 'heavy duty' wheels and tyres and a mid-mounted Zurcher engine. Mochet then incorporated a Ydral engine, as used in motorcycles, and built a car that was able to compete in a demanding market. His ability to create a very light vehicle reflected his pre-war pedal-car history. It was an improvement on his earlier crude Type-K that had been built since 1948, with its open bodywork and 50cc engine. The CM 175 Conduite Interieure saloon model with its two-stoke 175cc engine and three speeds was the apogee of the marque. By 1953, after production of the Luxe and the Grande Luxe, the market for small utility vehicles in rural France was growing. Mochet's short-lived Commerciale, or Camionette, was aimed at the butcher and the baker for a village delivery machine. In France, vehicles with a displacement of 125cc or less could be driven without a licence, thereby making the vans ideal for rural life.

The Sima-Violet was marketed as 'Le Cyclecar'. It was Monsieur Violet's légère or lightweight tandem seated cyclecar with a 500cc Sima opposed twin and an external flywheel. Jacques Potherat said their finest hour was at Arpajon in 1927, when they recorded a world record of 110.718kph. The photo is from the opening of the Miramas circuit in 1924.

A D'Yrsan, with a Y in its radiator to differentiate it from the X of Salmson. It was a sophisticated three-wheeler with its roots going back to the Sandford and the Morgan. It is photographed at Montlhéry in front of a two-wheeled car/motorcycle with outrigger wheels called the Monotrace, which had German ancestry in its design. This bizarre device was otherwise notable for having handlebar steering.

The Blériot Whippet one might assume, since it bore Louis Blériot's name, would have been made in France, but they were in fact made in a factory close to Blériot's British house at Addlestone in Kent. Designed by ex-employees of the Zenith motorcycle company, Messrs Jones and Marchant, it used the Zenith Gradua belt-drive system. The photograph shows over sixty cars at Addlestone.

A French-built Colombe with chain drive to the front wheel at Arpajon in 1924, going for 350cc records.

A Second World War deliveryman's device being utilised for a more formal occasion.

6
The Spacke and the Cyclecar in America

In the United States at the beginning of the twentieth century the dirt road was the norm and could be hard to negotiate when muddy, especially after the snow melted in the early spring. When it rained, ruts were created as the ground dried out. The towns all had roads of some description. In 1903 Detroit had almost 300 miles of paved roads made of cedar on concrete, cedar on planks, cedar on sand, brick on concrete, asphalt on concrete, granite on concrete, cobble on concrete, medina on concrete and macadam. Towns might have their internal roadways, but in the winter the connections between really important centres such as Baltimore, Philadelphia and Washington were sometimes a turmoil.

The farming community did not necessarily want better roads as there was often additional income to be earned by horses freeing cars that were immersed in quagmires. Farmers might not object to poor roads, but the business community needed good roads and hence the publicity attached to cross-America motoring attempts was welcome. The sixty-four day first crossing was noteworthy in 1903. In 1909 Alice Ramsay's efforts crossing Iowa, Wyoming and Utah in a Maxwell-Briscoe attracted major press coverage. The thirteen days she took to traverse Iowa's 360 miles of black heavy clay (known locally as Gumbo) was especially newsworthy.

In the first decade of the twentieth century it appeared there were several marketing opportunities for car manufacturers: for the farmer; for the town car; for the grand conveyance; for buggies. But there was also a need for a lightweight slim car that could keep out of the ruts and avoid the worst road horrors, and that was light enough to be man-handled if necessary.

A hundred cyclecar designs sprang up in all parts of the States and hosts of machines were announced. The buckboard was invented in the States as a fun machine in 1903, as A.O. Smith bought up the US rights of the British Wall Auto Wheel. This was used as a powered bolt-on fifth wheel, to mobilise the buckboard but the buckboard was not serious transport. Only ten or twelve cyclecars materialised, and they lasted but a short while. By the end of 1914, the beginning of 1915, the cyclecar craze was finished. But not before amazingly significant sums had been spent on designs with generally a higher engineering content than their European counterparts.

The premier motoring magazine of the Edwardian and the 1919 post-war period in the United States was *Motor Age*. The editor, William B. Stout, was also involved in manufacturing a cyclecar. He endeavoured to keep the editorial and car construction separate. He wrote in his non-Auburn Imp role and pronounced on 'America's Definition of the Cyclecar' in May 1913:

> *In the recently developed cyclecar – a four-wheeled motor-driven car reduced to its simplest and cheapest terms – lies the future hope of the masses for a fast, safe vehicle to carry them to and fro in cleanliness and comfort, at a cost within reach of the average purse. The new vehicle, now well developed abroad, is perfectly applicable to American conditions if correctly designed to meet*

these different requirements, and what criticisms have been directed against the possibilities of the new car for this country have been largely based on ignorance of the real significance of the movement.

A cyclecar in the spirit of the definition is a four-wheeled car built on the simplest motorcycle lines. This means all unnecessary parts are left off and only those put on that are absolutely necessary. A cheap car is thus produced which will do many of the things possible to higher priced cars at a greatly lowered first cost and upkeep. This is done without sacrificing either fine material or first class workmanship, the cheapness being obtained by design and refinement rather than by doing things sloppily.

In another article published in May 1913 and written on invitation 'by the Editor of the British magazine *Cyclecar*' was an article entitled 'The Cyclecar – England's Version':

The poor man's motor will, in all probability, be the pedal cycle and in Great Britain there must be well over 5,000,000 in use, the number being added to each year by part of an output that is estimated as not fewer than 500,000 annually. This year there is something in the nature of a famine in bicycles. The next stage is the autowheel, a little auxiliary motor wheel which trails alongside and slightly behind the bicycle to which it is attached and pushes it along. It seems likely to fill the gap between the bicycle and the motor cycle. The motor bicycle and the motor bicycle and sidecar are the next stages which bring us to the cyclecar, followed by what are known as miniature cars, light cars, and then the motor car proper, and of all of these various

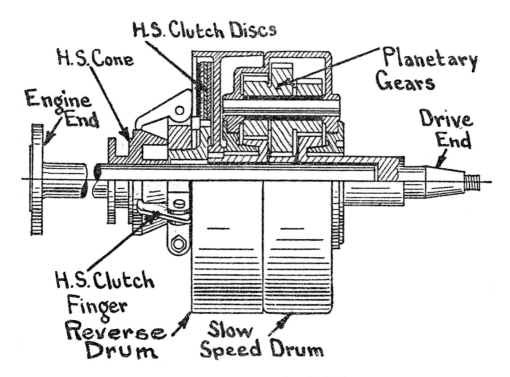

The two-speed and reverse epicyclic transmission system used on the Spacke.

means of mechanical progression, with the solitary exception of the pedal bicycle, the cyclecar seems likely to have by far and away the greatest number of devotees.

Every week sees the production of two or three more entirely new machines, some incorporating very novel ideas, others merely copies of big cars reduced to a small scale. Every week sees more and more of these machines on the road and on Saturdays and Sundays on each main highway from London at say 20 miles from town any number from half-a-dozen to a score will pass the onlooker in an hour.

The attention they create is astonishing. There is an active organisation known as the Cyclecar Club which holds rallies, runs and trials throughout the year, and at each of these motorists, motorcyclists and the non-motoring public collect in their hundreds, having come down to have a look at the wonderfully interesting little machines. It is impossible to leave a cyclecar, especially if it be what is known as the simple type, outside a hotel or restaurant while the owner goes inside for a meal without finding a big crowd collected around the machine when he emerges.

The public is filled with enthusiasm for the new movement and takes the keenest interest in the performances of the little machines. Some of these are small, compact and very comfortable, the replicas of big cars; others strike out on original lines with a more sporting appearance and with either chain or belt-drive, but the biggest baby in the cyclecar world and the one which is creating the most public interest is the monocar, or single-seated cyclecar. It has been predicted that this eventually will prove to be the biggest phase of the whole movement.

If the belt-driven type of machine is taken up in America the great point to bear in mind by manufacturers is that the rubber belts must not be less than 1⅛ inches wide nor less than 9 feet in length, while the front belt-pulleys must not be less than 6 inches in diameter and should preferably be 7 inchess or 8 inches. Rubber and canvas belts are the best here.

In the first 50 or 60 miles these belts will have the original stretch taken out of them and will require to be shortened 1½ to 2 inches. They should then run at least 2,000 miles without being touched, when they may require another shortening and should run at least 5,000 miles without being worn out. Indeed, experiences of 6,000 to 12,000 miles with belts is by no means uncommon. The belt fastener is the vulnerable point; spare fasteners should be carried, but better still, spare belts fitted with fasteners complete, as the task of slipping on a new belt is only a matter of a minute or so. In one respect the belt-driven type of machine has an advantage over any other in that it is exceedingly economical in regard to tyres.

In the opinion of many competent to judge, the three-wheeler will not have a very much longer vogue. The Morgan is the most successful, its low build and sporting appearance being important factors. Its transmission, from an air-cooled engine, is by carden shaft and a counter-shaft and then by chain on either side to the single driving wheel. It is a very successful machine and the fastest on the road, speeds of 50 miles per hour being easily maintained. It holds the hour record at Brooklands track for 59 miles 1,060 yards in the hour. The disadvantages are the inaccessibility of the back wheel and the great wear thereon, the three tracks instead of two.

The response to this new cult was the first issue of *The American Cyclecar*, published in July 1914 but unfortunately only a very few issues followed. Other publications featured the cyclecar such as *Light Car Age* and *Cyclecar Age*. There was an interesting letter in the very first issue of the *The American Cyclecar*, in which the writer asked for an explanation of 'the curious hostility to the cyclecar, that has developed and is being exploited, in the columns

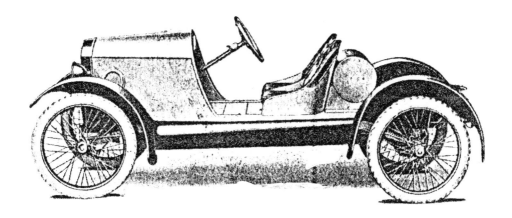

The Spacke was fitted with a front-mounted gravity fuel tank and the drum at the rear was for tools and personal equipment. In 1919 there was an optional fitting of a large case at the rear (at a cost of £5 in Britain) to convert the Spacke into a delivery van.

of the motor-cycling publications. The cyclecar is here to stay, and that fact might as well be recognised – both by the makers of high priced automobiles as well as the motor cycle manufacturers'.

One of the issues of a motorcycle journal editorially stated, 'This journal doesn't think the cyclecar in its present stage is adapted to American roads'. And further on, one of the leading articles has the prominent headline, 'Cyclecars Fail on American Roads', and then continues to say, 'We may well assume right at the start, that our American roads eliminate any car light enough to be in the cyclecar class, if personal comfort is to be taken into consideration.'

The cycle car became known in the United States in November 1913 when the Detroit Cycle Car and Motorette Club was founded at the Hotel Pontchartrain, Detroit. In January 1914, William B. Stout, father of the American cyclecar, was at the New York Auto Show with America's first cyclecar, the Imp, made in Auburn, Indiana. (No connection with the much later Auburn car).

Newspapers reported that the 'poor man's' car was here at last. One vehicle was powered through the left front wheel, which obviated 'the need for a differential'. There were inherent flaws with many of these machines. Many had hammock seats and no floor pan. If the hammock broke, the occupant could fall directly to the ground.

Steering was generally either rack and pinion or 'cotton reel', the American description of wire and bobbin, which was a 'drum connected to the tie rods and rope that wound around the steering shaft'. Seating was side by side, but mostly tandem in order to maintain a narrow track. It was reported that 'some had steering wheels in the back seat'. Most were powered by motorcycle engines, with drive belts that stretched and slipped. Frames were often made of wood 'that did not hold up'.

The Ford Model T had been designed and priced to meet the needs of the majority of customers, who happened to be farmers. Henry Ford was also interested in poor roads. The Model T could deal with poor roads, which were the same as the farmer's own farm tracks. The Ford Model T was steadily being reduced in price and approaching the cycle car in cost.

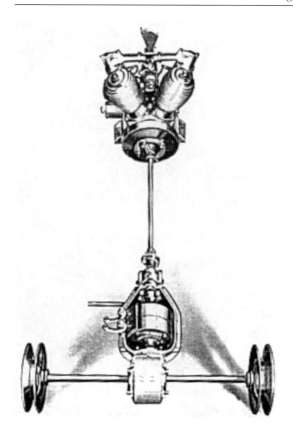

The Scripps-Booth used the Spacke engine which was fitted to a Spacke planetary gear at the trans-axle with belt drive to the rear axle. No recognition was made in print by Scripps-Booth as to the use of Spacke components.

In December of 1914 a Ford Model T was listed at $440, and cyclecars such as the Merz at $375 and the Trumbull at $395. Merz shortly afterwards launched their delivery vans onto the market with a four-cylinder engine, but retained the cyclecar friction drive transmission. The American car market was often confused by cars with remarkably similar names, such as the Metz, which had cyclecar ancestry.

Henry Ford was apprehensive that the cyclecar might succeed and he produced a lightweight Ford T stripped of luxury items. It is difficult to comprehend what actually he could take off such a basic motor car, but as Bob Casey, of the Ford Motor Museum said, referring to this model, 'that Henry Ford used it to scare off potential cycle-car producers.' The Roadster was the Ford T basic model and from 1912 through 1915 the price fell from $590, to $525, to $500 and finally to $440. At $440 it was only $50 more expensive than the average cyclecar.

In the American-built cyclecar, the early stages were the same as in Britain and France. The Bédélia system was copied by a number of American companies. Engines were available from any number of manufacturers such as The Wizard Motor Co., Mack and the Spacke Machine Co.; Wizard and Spacke were both of Indianapolis. Perry Mack built himself an automobile using an air-cooled engine and friction transmission of his own devising. Perry Mack was the designer of the air-cooled Mack engine being built by the Universal Machinery Co. of Milwaukee. The Mack truck which was in its infancy at that time had no connection with Perry Mack.

A typical specification of an air-cooled twin-cylinder American cyclecar would have the motor set fore and aft with a small chain sprocket on the extension of the crankshaft for the

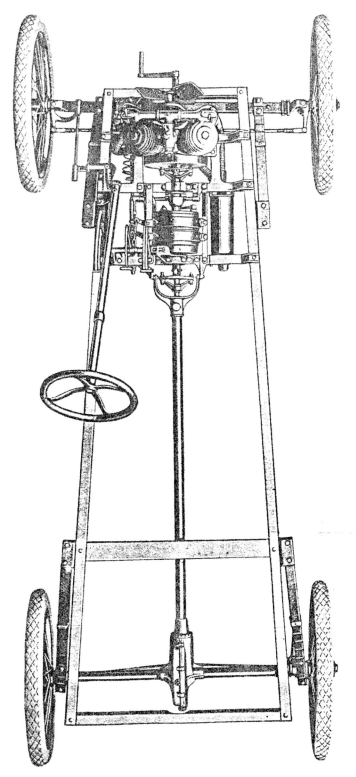

The Spacke chassis. The steering ratio is achieved by two gears in the open air. The back axle is of 6:1 gear driving the right-hand wheel, whilst the left-hand one coasts.

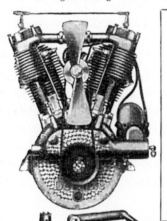

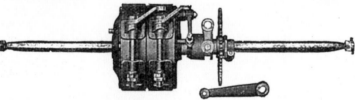
A Spacke advertisement of July 1914.

drive. From this a roller chain of motorcycle size carried the power back to the countershaft under the footboard of the driver's compartment. On each end of the countershaft, outside the body, a V-shape pulley was mounted. The pulleys lined up with similar but larger V-shape pulleys fastened directly to the rear wheels of the car. An owner of any European cyclecar would have followed this description. The two-speed action was obtained in many cases by a planetary gearset mounted on this countershaft and operated by pedals extending through the footboard of the car. In this way a clutch, two-speed, and reverse were obtained, without having to slacken off the rear axle.

The factories that got started quickly found that the public was interested and willing to watch their neighbour buy, but 'Joe Public' did not want to risk his money on experimental machines. Motorcycle motors were soon found to be too light and have too little flywheel to help tick-over situations. They were too noisy and too hard to start, exactly mirroring the same findings on the other side of the pond. Above all vee-twins cost more than a 'regular' four-cylinder motor. This last was the real vital reason for the discarding of the cyclecar idea in America – the abnormally high cost of V-type motors compared to an off-the-shelf four-cylinder side valve of 3-4 litres, and the fact that petrol was ludicrously cheap.

In mid 1914 the cyclecar boom was still in full swing, and the Zip Co. of Davenport in Iowa announced they were expanding production. An article entitled 'Cyclecar and Light Car Activities in Detroit' was published in *Automobile Trade Journal* in 1914. It reported:

> *The Scripps-Booth Cyclecar Company, of Detroit, has been shipping cars for several months, turning out as many as twenty in a single day. Some thirty cars are coming through each day, and are being shipped, according to Sales Manager Porter. It is the intention to have put out 5,600 of these cars by the close of the company's fiscal year, which is September.*

In the June issue of the *Automobile Trade Journal* was published a review of American light cars and cyclecars for 1914 and it had the following to say on the matter: 'There are some seventy

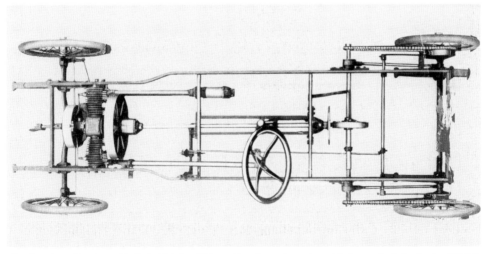

An American Greyhound built in Toledo, Ohio, with a flat twin engine with fore and aft flywheels of 1914. The driving disc of the friction drive is in the neutral position halfway across the driven disc.

plus other firms which are experimenting and perfecting models or laying them out on the drawing board.'

Scripps-Booth bought the De Luxe engine from Spacke but fitted their own rear axle gearbox and braking system. Scripps-Booth stated that the results of the cyclecar boom are apparent in the design of every big car that is now striving to lessen weight and add comfort, this desire being, to a certain extent, a result of cyclecar publicity. The Scripps-Booth Co., after a year's experiment with the cyclecar – built for minimum cost – jumped to the opposite extreme seeing that there was no future in cyclecars, and built an expensive luxurious car of extremely light weight on the belief that cars should be built lighter. They said, 'This new Scripps-Booth is being marketed in America with some slight success.'

A survey of 1914 represented the average and most popular constructions of all the cars on the market.

Price	$395
Passengers	two
Seating	side by side
Weight	665lb
Horsepower	$10\frac{3}{4}$ SAE
Cylinders	two (many did have four cylinders)
Bore	$3\frac{1}{8}$in
Stroke	$3\frac{3}{4}$in
Stroke to Bore Ratio	$1\frac{1}{4}$:1
Cooling	air, but water-cooled cars were built
Transmission	friction
Speeds Forward	two
Gear Ratio	$23\frac{1}{4}$in per revolution of engine
Drive	belt
Tires	28in x 3in
Driver's Position	left side
Front Springs	semi-elliptic
Tread	$42\frac{1}{2}$in
Rear Springs	cantilever
Wheel base	$96\frac{3}{4}$in

There was a marked difference in the exchange rate between the US Dollar and Pound Sterling. Pre-1914 the $425 US cyclecar would have been equivalent to £55 in Britain at roughly $8 to £1. The cost of shipping and duties would have considerably increased this beyond £55, inhibiting the saturation of the market.

Competition between makes found favour on the racetrack. 10,000 people saw the first cyclecar race in America at Detroit in July 1914 with twenty-eight entries. Coey in the Coey Bear dominated the meeting and the Morgan, which was a Grand Prix model with the water-cooled ninety-bore high compression JAP engine was credited as being easily the fastest machine and 'made a killing' in the Class A and short distance free-for-alls. In October 1914, there was a light car race at Medford, Massachussetts, as a prelude to the Light Car and Cyclecar Show in Boston. During the big race of the day, which was a 50k free-for-all, many of the cars broke down, shed components and the winner made it with a flat front tyre. The

SHAW SPEEDSTERS are all equipped with 2½ H. P. SHAW BICYCLE MOTORS. Carrying Capacity 500 lbs.

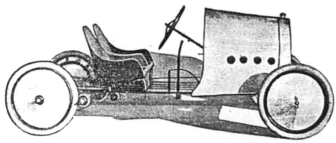

Model 6B battery ig
nition ....$138.0(

Model 5B same a:
Model 6B except witl
wire wheels and 20
inch single tube bi
cycle tires........$125.0(

Model 6M magneto igni-
tion $151.00

Model 5M same as Model 6M
except with wire wheels and
20-inch single tube bicycle
tires $138.00

Model 3B battery igni-
tion $133.00

Model 2B same as Model 3B except with wire wheels and 20-
inch single tube bicycle
tires $120.00

Model 3M Magneto
ignition $146.00

Model 2M same as Model 3M
except with wire wheels and
20-inch single tube bicycle
tires $133.00

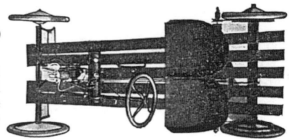

OUR GUARANTEE!

We AGREE to make good by repair or replacement within one year from date of invoice, any defect in material or workmanship of any Shaw Speedster, provided the defective part is delivered to us, transportation prepaid. This guarantee does not cover any damage by accidents, misuse or neglect.

SHAW MANUFACTURING CO.

Buckboards could be built to specification.

Possibly an American Cameron of 1914. A four-cylinder water-cooled cyclecar demonstrating the narrowness of track, which was a built-in requirement to work your way around poor roads.

fairgrounds in the US were the scene of most of the races and entrants of Twomblys and others must have looked askance at the Morgan entered by Richard Allen, and the car scored easy wins.

In America there was an interest in cyclecars and three-wheeled vehicles for delivery purposes. These were developed by both cyclecar and motorcycle firms. The Indian and Harley-Davidson firms built what became known as delivery tricars. The Harley-Davidson delivery tricar mounted the motor in the frame as on a motorcycle, but in front of the handlebar a large box was fitted with wheels on either side and had an axle running underneath, to which the body was connected by flat leaf springs. The front axle connected back to the rear axle of the motorcycle part by pressed steel side frame members, which made the construction rigid and strong. This parcel van was fitted with a two or three-speed gear, to make it capable of a wide range of activity.

The cyclecar manufacturers who survived for a time were Imp, Zip, Briggs & Stratton with a buckboard and Spacke (pronounced in the US as 'spak-ee'). The F.W. Spacke Machine Co. manufactured automobile engines and components. The business prospered; and a good many of the cyclecars of the 1914-1915 era were fitted with Spacke engines. In 1917 the new Spacke made by a new company, the Spacke Machine & Tool Co., offered the pre-war engine, the two-cylinder air-cooled 9/13hp unit, developing 14bhp at 2,500rpm. The wheelbase was 90in, the tread 46in, and the only body style offered was a $295 roadster with two bucket seats. For the 1920 model year the car was redesignated the Brook. They marketed products under both Spacke and De Luxe. Spacke with very little competition from other American cyclecar firms promoted themselves in Europe, using the names of Spacke and De Luxe, but with almost no success. How many clients Spacke had is not known, but the following cyclecar producers in America used their fifty-five degree vee-twin air-cooled inlet over exhaust 1,150cc engine with its cooling fan – Puritan, Mercury, Scripps-Booth, Falcon, Crickett, Fenton, Arrow, and Greyhound – and probably countless others for their prototypes.

The Spacke Co. started as a supplier of components to cyclecar manufacturers. Epicyclic transmission as used in the Ford Model T was well understood so the Spacke transmission of two forward gears and a reverse by bands where emergency retardation could be obtained in the same way as a Trojan by forcing the gear lever into first or even reverse to supplement the foot brake, also working on the gearbox. There was no handbrake as such; the system allowed the foot brake to be locked whereupon it served the purpose of a hand brake. Final drive was via the right hand rear wheel only and hence the back axle had no need for a differential.

The Spacke engine was cheap and lightweight and typified the cyclecar industry of America. The construction was claimed to be beefier than engines fitted into a motorcycle and the motor itself was hung in a cast frame, which carried also a countershaft on ball bearings. Several constructions that used the Spacke engine had next to the motor, on a large ball bearing, a friction disc, which connected direct to the motor shaft by means of a flexible pin joint coupling. This enabled a lever operated by a pedal to move the disc forward and backward to bring it into contact with a friction wheel faced with fibre, and arranged to slide back and forth on a countershaft. Thus a friction gearset of simplicity, not dissimilar to the British GWK, was obtained, allowing a four-speed change between the motor and the pulley transmission. The belts ran from vee-pulleys on either side of the car. They were very long

This 1914 press photograph was staged by the Mercury Cyclecar Co. of Detroit. Mercury was a cyclecar pioneer using the Spacke engine, friction transmission with final drive by vee-belt. Mercury started production in March 1914 and were petitioned into bankruptcy in September of the same year. The three Mercury cars were photographed in a Detroit suburb, demonstrating that Mercury thought they were here to stay.

$385
F. O. B. OWEGO

O-WE-GO
Cyclecars

COMPLETE WITH ALL
EQUIPMENT
EXCEPT TOP

Light weight and economy of upkeep, combined with perfect comfort in riding on rough roads, speed and ample power for steep hills, are essential features of O-WE-GO Cyclecars.

We are now making stock deliveries of both the two-passenger model and the light delivery car.

The two-passenger roadster is a graceful, beautifully finished cyclecar, electric lighted and equipped, with glass windshield, horn and tools, and sells for $385.

The delivery model is fitted with the same equipment, including a full panel steel body and top, and sells for $405. Write for catalog and our selling plan.

O-WE-GO CAR COMPANY, OWEGO, TIOGA CO., N. Y.
442 FRONT STREET

The American Sinclair Millitor three-passenger 'car' was a variant development of the motorcycle/sidecar. The chassis was a single steel pan pressing incorporating the sump, bottom of the gearbox and the base of the front and rear suspensions.

and carried the power to the rear wheels. No axles, as we know them today, were fitted, but instead parallel cross springs were mounted front and rear, with spindles on either and holding the wheels, so that the only unsprung weight on the car was that of the wheels.

It was reported in the press that 10,000 two-cylinder Imps were made. The Imp had a 100in wheelbase and 36in track, and seated the passengers in tandem in a very low, narrow body, similar to the Bédélia. The Imp was advertised in the British *Light Car and Cyclecar* magazine with a two-page advertisement by the distributor, prior to the First World War, priced at £98. The motor was set crosswise in front with the shaft running fore and aft, thus allowing of the motor to be started by using a crank at the front end as in conventional automobiles.

By the end of 1914, bankruptcies amongst cyclecar producers were being listed. The Mercury Cyclecar of Detroit going under in October of 1914. Recognising the changing times the magazine title *American Cyclecar* was changed in 1915 to *The Carette and the American Cyclecar* and shortly afterwards became *The Carette*. It was practically all over for cyclecars. The export market beckoned. Owego, Twombly, Spacke and the Imp were all active selling in Britain in 1914, but with seemingly no success. Dudley of Michigan claimed to have exported cars to Spain. France imposed import duties in the post-1918 years, but it was a lost cause for the American cyclecar, as Henry Ford had had his ruthless way. But he who lives by the sword can also equally be harmed by it; the sophisticated 490 Chevrolet sold for $490 in 1916. Chevrolet had applied the same low price lesson as Ford, with a much more up to date specification and design.

The cyclecar was not wholly dead, for the Spacke organisation built up an export business, but reformed itself as the Brook cyclecar, and in 1922 moved to Trenton, New Jersey, to be made as the Peters, but the Spacke disappeared soon afterwards. The manufacturers of buck-boards, such as the Red Bug with a battery-driven electric motor, also survived and went on being produced until the late 1920s.

In 1919 the reformed and re-sited Spacke company scrapped their perfectly effective epicyclic transmission and fitted a conventional gearbox with transmission brake drum and a hand brake.

Above: *A Twombly in Shanghai.*

The Twombly Light Underslung Car

$395

A cyclecar only in tread---really a perfect small automobile. All the power plant covered by original patents granted to Mr. Twombly---motor transmission and rear axle. Engine free from all cam shaft and timing gear complications; self-started. Four cylinders, water-cooled, thermo-siphon. Twombly patents on underslung system---with a center of gravity lower than that of any car now built. Twombly three-step friction transmission giving six speeds forward and two reverse. Twombly live rear axle with differential

$395

A Miniature Automobile

Live Rear Axle

Tandem (2)
Roadster (2)
Raceabout (1)
Delivery

Pressed Steel Frame Channel Section

Fully Equipped

Underslung

Factory Avondale, N. J.

100-inch Wheel Base

9-inch Clearance

Fully Guaranteed

I-Beam Front Axle Drop-Forged Chrome

40 Miles to the gallon of gas

Speed 50 Miles an Hour

Bosch Magneto

Schebler Carburetor

28x2½-inch Wire Wheels

38-in. tread

Weight 600 lbs.

unbreakable type, solid shaft from wheel to wheel, with differential casing operating as emergency brake. Springs, 36-inch cantilever rear; 30-inch semi-elliptic front Telescopic steering gear, adjustable to suit bulk of driver.

$395

Price $395, f. o. b. Factory

$395

The Twombly factory is running night and day. We shall have two Twomblys at the Boston show. We shall commence deliveries April 1.

H. ROSS MADDOCKS COMPANY, Inc., *Distributors*
175 Pleasant Street, Boston   Boston Show Spaces { Pleasure, No. 255 / Truck, Nos. 24 and 25

ALSO DISTRIBUTORS OF STEWART DELIVERY TRUCKS

FALCON—$385
Falcon Cyclecar Co., Cleveland, O.

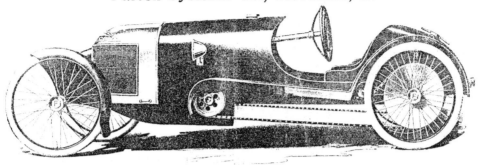

Motor—9-13 horsepower Spacke	Final drive—V belts	Seating—Side-by-side
Two cylinder V, 3.5 by 3.67 in.	Springs—Front, double transverse	Wheelbase—96 in.
Air cooled	Rear, inverted transverse	Tread—36 in.
A-K or magneto ignition	Wheels—Wire	Tires—28 by 3 in.
Displacement, 70.6 cu. in.	Frame—Tubular	Weight—375 lbs.
Transmission—Friction	Body—Metal	

The Falcon was fitted with a Spacke engine and a chain drive.

CRICKETT—$385
Crickett Cyclecar Co.   Detroit, Mich.

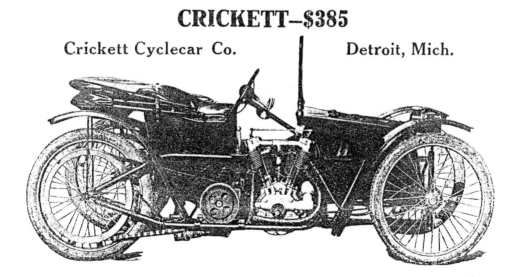

The Crickett was clearly designed for ex-motorcyclists who had never seen a car.

WHAT OTHERS SAY

THE FIRST CYCLECAR IN AMERICA

BUILT BY VEHICLE BUILDERS OF FORTY FIVE YEARS EXPERIENCE

Our Facilities for Manufacturing in Volume
are Unlimited and Our Proposition to the
Dealer is a "LIVE AND LET LIVE" One

OUR CYCLECAR IS THE SIMPLEST SELF PRO-PELLED VEHICLE THAT WAS EVER PRODUCED

All Our Vehicles are Sold Under a Standard
Warrant for One Year

It Will Please You to Own the First Cycle Car

IMP CYCLECAR CO.
AUBURN, INDIANA

The American Imp cyclecar, shown above in the Henry Ford Museum, was built by William Stout and owes a lot to the Spacke company.

7
Cars after the Second World War and the Microcar

After the First World War, the Treaty of Versailles expressly forbade German aircraft manu-facturers from building aeroplanes. This caused the manufacturers to look at other ways of keeping their factories busy, including car and motorcycle manufacture. After 1945 the same thinking about the possibility of car design and production in the German aeronautical industry was paramount. The Lloyd 300 of 1947 was more sophisticated than post-1918 cars when it was made in Bremen and earned the delightful nickname of the Leukoplastbomber – 'sticky plaster bomber'. The Lloyd went through some redesigns and soon became a small car with a good appearance

One of the most famous of the post-war microcars was the Messerschmitt. Fritz Fend, its designer, worked for Messerschmitt on the jet-engined powered Me262 fighter during the latter days of the war. He built his first car in 1947, a pedal-powered Flitzer. Fend argued that non-essential materials could well be released for such a device to move the injured around; the War Wounded Association was interested, and materials might be forthcoming. The resulting small three-wheeled tricycle had a seat in the middle and a control lever with

"Three times I asked the fellow what it was, and all he did was stutter."

Russell Brockbank, as the doyen of motoring cartoonists, regularly poked fun at the post-war microcars. For today's audience the car that stuttered is the Goggo.

A Goggomobil TS400 coupe in right hand drive form. This early car has suicide doors and the 400cc engine.

handlebars in front. Pushing and pulling the control lever powered the car, steering was via the handlebars. The interest that was hoped for did not materialise, but the War Wounded Association ordered fifty, and so began the construction of cars to Fend's designs.

At the time, the German aircraft industry was full of diversification ideas and the aircraft firm of Dornier designed a car (originally called the Dornier Delta), with back-to-back seating. Zundapp manufactured a variant under licence as the Janus. Before the Janus came on the market there was the Isetta, originally based on the Iso design but greatly improved and made more reliable by BMW. Hans Glas produced the Goggomobil after a spell manufacturing scooters and agricultural equipment. His Goggomobil in one development form used an electrically preset gearbox and a 250cc two-stroke twin. Glas survived into the late 1960s until the firm was taken over by BMW who wanted the factory space for increased production of their own cars. The Heinkel Kabine bubble top was inspired by the BMW Isetta and the design was licensed and sold all over the world, being manufactured in Ireland by Dundalk Engineering and in Britain by the Trojan Co. of Croydon and sold under their name.

In the UK, post-1945, the Labour Government took drastic economic measures, including the rationing of petrol until 1950. Import quotas were enforced and the allocation of scarce raw materials, such as steel, went only to industries that could guarantee export potential. In 1948 the first post-war Motor Show was held, with little chance for Joe Public to buy anything, as over sixty per cent of motor vehicle production was directed by the Government for export.

It was recognised in those difficult times, as it had been post-1918, that there was a need for a very basic type of vehicle. Desirable features would include construction in a relatively

Hans Glas' Goggomobil van. Again this is a real rarity today but these vans were once a common sight on Germany's roads. It was powered by the same two stroke twin as the saloon and coupe.

This rather dilapidated Zundapp Janus was found in Sweden in 1993.

cheap and plentiful material that was not subject to any restrictions. The new road tax laws came into force on 1 January 1948. These new laws saw the replacement of the old RAC horsepower rating system, with a flat rate annual fee of £10, but three-wheelers were only liable for half that amount.

A number of attempts were made in Britain to rival the post-war French and German developments in ultra light vehicles or microcars, as they tended to be known. The word cyclecar was too dated, but due to the grasping tendencies of the British Treasury there were no dispensations of Road Fund taxation, as customers in continental Europe could expect for lightweight vehicles. The main impetus in Britain for microcars came from Lawrie Bond, who having been in the British aviation industry, produced the first Bond Minicar in 1947. The Bond Minicar was manufactured in Preston by Sharp's Commercials, a refurbisher of ex-army trucks, and was to be manufactured in various models until 1968.

The Isetta

In 1953, Renzo Rivolta of Milan began constructing the Isetta. In 1955 he sold the rights of manufacture to BMW. BMW replaced the original two-stroke engine with an air-cooled 247cc, single-cylinder, four-stroke. It sat at the back of the car and drove the rear wheels via a gearbox and enclosed chain. BMW also redesigned the car's suspension. The body was mounted on a tubular chassis. There were two rear wheels set just 48cm apart. In 1956 a 295cc engine was introduced for export models. The '300' had changes to the body style. The front-opening door was a novelty but practical. The universally jointed steering column and instrument binnacle swung providing a clear access to the interior.

A BMW Isetta 300 sliding window model.

This BMW Isetta is a 250cc bubble window model from 1956. The universal-jointed steering column is shown to effect here.

In 1957, a four-passenger '600' version with a 585cc flat-twin engine was introduced. Access to the rear seats was via a right rear side door.

Isettas were made under licence in, among other places, France, Brazil and in Brighton, England. Parts arrived from BMW in Germany to the redundant Pullman Carriage Works in Brighton and were assembled on a single production line, with a 'siding' into and out of the paint shop. At the end of the line, twenty-five new Isettas at a time would await train transport out to dealerships. It was probably the first and only car factory with no vehicular road access. Customers who preferred to do so could collect their car from their local railway station (pre-Beeching), with almost zero delivery mileage.

When the Brighton factory began production it already had an advance order for 1,000 cars for export to Canada. In addition to the basic Isetta car, the Brighton works also produced a pick-up truck with fabric roof, which as a small delivery van was popular on the continent. The RAC used some within the UK as did other firms, keen to have a small van for local deliveries. As a *Motor* road test pointed out, the Isetta 'is willing to go anywhere and do anything, and the manner of its going entertains some people very much indeed.'

Messerschmitt

From the small beginnings of the Fend Flitzer grew the most famous of the postwar microcars, the Messerschmitt. Fritz Fend went to his one-time boss, Willy Messerschmitt, and showed him his designs for a new form of car. They discussed the car that they would build. It would be a three-wheeled, two-seater, with the passenger sitting behind the driver. A plexiglass canopy would offer weather protection and would be hinged at one side so that it could be lifted to give access to the cabin. The new car would be powered by a 150cc engine. The two men were convinced that they had a successful design, so a proper partnership was formed in 1952. It was named the 'Fend Kabinenroller' type FK150. The public were able to buy the car from 1953, when it was displayed at the Geneva motor show. It immediately attracted sporting drivers but due to its narrow track it could be unstable if driven hard. A higher-powered version, the Kr175 appeared soon after. In 1955 a totally new model, along similar lines to the Kr175, was unveiled to the public. This was the Kr200, with a Fichtel & Sachs 191cc engine, electric start (via a dynastart – effectively a dynamo and starter all in one neat package), 12V electrics and room for two adults and one child.

Messerschmitts were lighter than the competitive bubble cars and had a sporting appearance. The narrow track meant that it was sometimes possible to lift a wheel when spirited cornering was indulged in. If the driver ignored this symptom then it was ridiculously simple to end up upside-down in the roadside ditch.

The four-wheeled FMR Tg500 had a top speed of over 80mph and had superb handling.

The significant change for the Kr200 was that a second pair of points were installed in the ignition circuit, so that if reverse were required the ignition was switched off and the second pair of points selected (via a solenoid), which were at a retard setting. Hence when the engine was turned over it would fire backwards and the engine running backwards thereby provided reverse in all the four gears. The ordinarily very stable Messerschmitt was lethal going backwards and various drivers attempted high-speed reverses and ended up with their car turned over. It was said by other microcar owners that there were more dead Messerschmitt car drivers in the cemeteries than Messerschmitt fighter pilots from the war. However, the car continued to be just as popular as ever, even as more competition from other small cars affected the market. Fend prepared a much modified Kr200 and on 29 August 1955 made a record attempt at Hockenheim circuit in a twenty-four hour test. The lap average settled down at around 106kph; 60mph for a 200cc car continuously was no mean achievement.

The ultimate development of the Messerschmitt concept was the FMR Tiger, which was a true four wheeler, with a 500cc engine based on a Sachs design but built by the company. The manufacturing name of Messerschmitt was abandoned in favour of FMR Tg500 – the Tg standing for Tiger and the FMR for Fahrzeug und Maschinenbau, GmbH of Regensburg. To this day the Messerschmitt models are highly regarded.

Another stylish Tg500. Independent suspension, speed and handling saw this model used for racing and rallying in the 1960s. They even had their own series of races at the Nurburgring in the 1970s.

The Kr200 was a highly successful model with over 38,000 sold. It was sold as a mini sports car, and had a 67mph top speed, or so the adverts claimed!

Available in soft top, as sports, roadster and cabriolet, the Messerschmitt was always better without the dome top, which boiled the occupants in summer and still leaked when it rained. Here is a late 1950s cabriolet.

The Kr200 was available in a variety of models: dome top, cabriolet, roadster and sports model. Arrangements of side and tail lamps varied depending on the country of export. British buyers had side lights on the front wings and four tail lamps, causing great strain on their 90 Watt Siba or Bosch Dynastart systems, especially when it rained and the wipers were on as well.

Despite its primitive looks, the Spanish-built Voisin Biscuter found 5,500 purchasers. Its Villiers engine had a huge heatsink head to cope with Spanish weather.

Heinkel and Trojan

In 1955 Heinkel of Stuttgart introduced a three-wheeled car, called the Kabine (Cabin Cruiser) which was similar in appearance to the BMW Isetta and powered by a 174cc single-cylinder four-stroke engine. However, unlike the Isetta, the Kabine had no chassis but relied on a stressed skin body.

A 204cc engine was introduced in 1956 and, at the same time, twin rear wheels were installed. The interior design of the Heinkel offered room for two adults at the front and two children in the rear. The front opening door hinged at the side, although the steering column was fixed rather than lifting with the door. There was a possibility of parking head-on to the kerb, as the car's length was less than the width of a more conventional vehicle; however, if the kerbstone was high then this method of parking was not practical. It was considered by many as the prettiest of the bubblecars; it had graceful lines and presented a friendly face to the world. It was also very practical and frugal.

The Heinkel was produced in Germany, in left-hand drive form only, until 1958 when a production licence was sold to Dundalk Engineering in Northern Ireland. Dundalk added a convertible version to its production which was, again, totally left hand drive. There was also some small-scale manufacture in Argentina.

In 1962 Trojan of Croydon began to make the car under their own name as the 'Trojan 200'. In all, over 6,000 Trojans were made, in both left and right-hand drive.

Left: *The Trojan, like many microcars, was advertised as cheaper than walking. Even holidays were inexpensive – although, the week to get to Spain and the week back might just have spoiled the fortnight's break!*

Above: *The Powerdrive was one of those British attempts to make a real sized car with microcar qualities. At 13ft long, with a steel chassis and aluminium body, its fan-cooled, 322cc British Anzani engine was lucky to push it into the forties. Only approximately twenty-one were made and perhaps five survive today, only one in original running order. Its designer went on to make the Coronet, a glassfibre convertible, loosely based on the Powerdrive.*

The Bond

It was Lawrie Bond who was the key player in the post-war British scene. Lawrence 'Lawrie' Bond was the designer and originator of Britain's most successful post-1945 microcar, the Bond Minicar. In the mid-1930s Lawrie Bond was working in the drawing office of Meadows Engineering Ltd in Wolverhampton. From there he went on to work for the Blackburn Aircraft Co. at Brough, where he stayed throughout most of the war. By 1944 Lawrie Bond had set up the Bond Aircraft & Engineering Co. (Blackpool) Ltd. By the end of the 1940s the Bond Aircraft & Engineering Co. had moved to new premises at Towneley Works, Berry Lane, Longridge, Lancashire. His work not only included the design of the Berkeley, the Opperman Unicar and the BAC Gazelle scooter. He also was a Formula III car builder with a front-engined JAP engine, at the time when the rear-engined Cooper was already dominating the Formula III racing class.

The prototype Bond Minicar fitted the politically motivated utility requirements of the time and it aroused considerable interest when it was first announced early in 1948. The mainly aluminium construction gave the prototype the remarkably low dry weight of 195lb. Lawrie Bond entered into an agreement in 1948 that Sharps Commercials Co. of Preston would take over the manufacturing rights, but would retain him as a consultant.

The Mk A Bond Minicar power was provided by a 122cc, Villiers Mk 10D, single cylinder, two-stroke motorcycle engine with an integral three-speed gearbox, which was claimed to produce 5bhp at 4,400rpm. The manufacturers claimed 49bhp per ton unladen. The gearbox did not incorporate a reverse gear, but there was the added advantage that the holder of a motorcycle licence was entitled to drive the Minicar without having to pass a car driving test.

One feature that the early Minicar shared with its cyclecar predecessors was the use of the cable and bobbin method of steering. Sharp's Commercials designed a simple rack and pinion system to update the design and introduced it early on. They had problems with the original Mk A's steering sticking on full lock. A kick to the engine frame and tube was often enough to cure this basic problem – until the next time! Sharps Commercials also realised that such developments in the design of a Minicar were of considerable interest to existing owners, as well as potential future owners. This was a policy that would be continued with later developments, which enabled owners to update their vehicles at least to a limited degree, but it was still a trend that few other vehicle manufacturers were likely to want to emulate.

Lawrie Bond helped with some work on the development of the Mk A and also the transition to the Mk B Minicar. Granville Bradshaw, a legendary figure in car design from the 1920s, occasionally did work for the firm including the design of the rear suspension for the Mk B Minicar, using a flexitor unit, which was similar to today's Indispension units and comprised a stub axle held in rubber in torsion. The original Mk A had used its balloon tyres to provide suspension.

The De Luxe Mk A in 1950 featured a larger 197cc Villiers Mk 6E engine. This De Luxe model was priced at £262 13*s* 11*d* and featured an electric windscreen wiper. Production had reached around forty vehicles per week and the demand was such that delivery time was quoted at five to six months. A curved 'Triplex' safety glass windscreen with improved cast aluminium windscreen pillars to take the extra weight was also introduced. A small starter

A Bond MkB at Morecambe, scene of many a club rally in the 1950s and home today to the Bond Owners Club International Rally.

MICHELIN

STRONG, SILENT SUPPLE and SAFE!

-the tyre for the BOND MINICAR

motor was fitted which drove a vee-belt onto the rim of the fly-wheel magneto. The Mk C Minicar was announced in September 1952 with limited production commencing in October. At the 1952 motorcycle show there were now three manufacturers of three-wheelers exhibiting. The Reliant Regal, introduced in 1951, and the AC Petite, but the Bond still held the price advantage. Advertising of the model inferred that it was cheaper to run than walking!

Production of the C Minicar began in January 1952. It featured large dummy front wings, which incorporated the headlamps. These were added not for purely decorative purposes, but to allow for sufficient room for the front-wheel drive unit to turn 180 degrees from lock to lock. The Mk C had the ability to be literally turned round in its own diagonal length, a feature that was to become a trade mark of the Bond Minicars, since a car not needing a reverse meant that the Minicar could continue to be driven on a motorcycle licence, without the disadvantage of having to get out and push. A new bulkhead assembly comprising a full-width aluminium casting in place of the braced aluminium structure strengthened the structure of the vehicle. The new body design included an opening passenger side door (as fitted to a few of the last Mk Bs) and the use of glass fibre for the first time for the rear wings (mainly on Family four/five-seat models) and some bonnets.

A De Luxe model with a more sophisticated electric starter (actually a starter motor bolted to the top of the cylinder head with a belt drive to the flywheel) and front and rear chrome bumpers was fitted. New variants included the Minitruck, a light commercial version with a single seat and a hood that featured a roll-up flap at the rear. A new family model was also based on the Mk C. This featured the same extended rear body section as the Minitruck. The Family model was fitted with two sideways-facing hammock seats suitable for two young children and accessed by clambering over the front bench seat. As the Family model used the same bench seat as the Standard and De Luxe models (which it was claimed could accommodate three people) the new model was advertised as a five seater! In late 1953 the company included the fitting of a new high output generator and magneto unit. This also included the fitting of a charge-rate control switch on the dashboard, with a high rate for night driving. The Mk C Minicars were promoted with full-colour sales brochures replacing the old single-colour, leaflet-style literature used previously. The Mk C continued until 1956, with around 6,700 having been built. The Mark D uplifted the various components and styling only in minor matters. The main change was the fitting of a Villiers 9E engine with SIBA Dynastart and 12V electrics in place of the Villiers 8E with magneto and 6V electrics. Stirling Moss described his experiences driving a Family Model Minicar through heavy London traffic which was published in a Bond promotional leaflet; it was not at all clear as to which sector of the car buying public this leaflet was directed.

Three models were announced in 1958 with the F range, based on the short-lived Mk E's larger bodyshell, but with a 246cc engine instead of the under-powered 197cc Villiers 9E of the Mk E. The new models were a three-seat tourer, a four-seat family saloon with a glass fibre roof and two small hammock seats in the rear, suitable for two children, and a three-seat saloon coupé. Sharp's also continued manufacturing the Mk D family saloon.

A 246cc Villiers Mk31A engine with its four-speed gearbox, gave the Mk F a respectable top speed of 55mph. It was fitted with the SIBA Dynastart unit as standard, with an optional reverse. By April 1959 production had reached almost 100 Minicars a week. Two commercial models of the Mk F were available from 1960 – the Ranger and the Minivan (identical but with no passenger seat fitted).

Advertising of the microcar tended to concentrate on fuel consumption and safety as well as any sporting pretensions. These ads are just typical of the period and of the cars themselves.

7,000 Mk Fs were built and it was probably the most popular and practical Minicar that Sharp's built. The Mk G range of Minicars were to be the last of the line for Sharp's Commercials, since by the late 1950s the economic factors and various restrictions that had given the earlier models such a boost had now almost completely disappeared.

The economy Mk G Tourer model failed to revive sales, although production of Mk G Minicars did continue as late as 1966, but only to order, and with just over 3,000 Mk G vehicles built, the Minicar story came to a close. Bond made brave attempts to live with the major manufacturers and manufactured various models of the Bond Equipe (based on Triumph Herald and Vitesse underpinnings).

After fifteen years of continuous production, with some 26,500 minicars having rolled off the production line, it was time for change. The recently appointed managing director of Sharp's Commercials, Tom Gratrix, had already seen the danger signs and as early as 1962 plans were being discussed, not only for a replacement three-wheeler, but also the possibility of entering the four-wheel specialist sports car market. It was not practical, however, and it was all over. The company was sold to Reliant, who almost instantly stopped production of the Hillman Imp-based Bond 875, thus ending the manufacture of Bond three wheelers. In the early 1970s the Bond name was revived for the Bond Bug, an orange cheese wedge, based on a Reliant Regal chassis and powered by Reliant's own engine.

The Berkeley

The Berkeley was designed by Lawrie Bond for Charles Panter of Berkeley Coachwork Ltd and built by Berkeley Cars Ltd at Biggleswade in Bedfordshire. It first appeared in 1956. The company had experience of glass fibre in the construction of caravans and the Berkeley car

The Berkeley T60 was the most successful of all Berkeleys with over 1,700 manufactured.

The accommodation of a Berkeley. The motorcycle ancestry is clear from the gear lever only operating in one vertical plane. Location of the spare wheel was under the dashboard.

was a means of keeping the staff employed during the slack time caused by the seasonal sales pattern of caravan retailing. The Berkeley was of semi-monocoque construction in glass fibre with steel and aluminium strengthening tubes and box sections bonded into the shell. It was the lightest and smallest four-wheel car on the market that combined sports car performance with economy. John Bolster tested the car for *Autosport*, recording an average fuel consumption of over 50mpg, with a top speed of 70mph and all for a price of under £600. The car boasted all-round independent suspension using helical springs and telescopic dampers made by Girling (who also provided the excellent hydraulic brakes). The front-mounted engine was a tuned 322cc air-cooled Anzani vertical twin with a rotary inlet valve. Transmission was by chain to the three-speed Albion gear-box with reverse, a three-plate, oil bath clutch was used with a secondary chain-drive to a spur-type differential and final-drive to the front wheels via Hardy-Spicer universally-jointed halfshafts. The performance was good which led to competition use of the car.

The Berkeley was built with either the Anzani engine (the first 168 cars) or a 328cc Excelsior Talisman Twin engine. In 1957 a more powerful engine was designed by Lawrie Bond. This was a modified Excelsior engine, which in effect used three-cylinder barrels from the Talisman Twin engine to make a two-stroke three-cylinder engine.

Development of the new three-cylinder 492cc engine was taken up by the Excelsior Motorcycle Co. and it was soon being built specifically for the Berkeley. Various versions of the car continued to be built through to 1961, and these included an extended four-seater – the B90 Foursome in 1958 – and a three-wheel version, the T60, in 1959. There were also more powerful models using the 692cc Royal Enfield Super Meteor and Constellation engines, designated the B95 and B105 respectively (this was supposed to indicate the top speed of the model concerned). Berkeleys did enjoy limited success in competition, and Count Johnny Lurani raced three special Berkeley SE492s at Monza, winning against more powerful Fiat Abarths.

By 1961, cash flow problems and a spate of warranty claims from American purchasers saw the company go in to liquidation. Development work on the Berkeley Bandit (a Ford-based sports model) also used up much of the company's cash reserve. A merger between Berkeley Cars Ltd and Sharp's Commercials Ltd, manufacturers of the Bond, was not considered a viable proposition and Berkeley Cars Ltd folded. Various efforts were made to revive the company but to no avail.

The Frisky and the Peel

There were many strange devices produced in Britain in the period of the microcar, such as the Peel P50 and Trident models made in the Isle of Man from 1962. Peel were in business with car prototypes for practically twenty years, some of the later ones were good looking and sporty. However, the Trident and P50 were not among them.

The Trident with a maximum length of 4ft 2in and a 49cc DKW engine was their only vehicle produced in number. Fewer than eighty cars were built. It was a lively model and frugal in operation.

Henry Meadows (Vehicles) Ltd, was well known as manufacturers in the vintage years of the 1,500, 3,000 and 4,500cc engines fitted to many British cars, but they had never been anything other than a supplier of engines and gearboxes to the British car industry. In the 1920s and the 1930s they supplied engines and gearboxes to Frazer Nash, Invicta, Lagonda and Lea-Francis. Their first venture as a car manufacturer was the four-wheeled, gull-winged prototype of the Frisky, designed by Raymond Flower and 'styled' by Michelotti. The Frisky's equipment was basic. All that came as standard was a speedometer, although a rev counter and fuel gauge could be bought, and there was a luxury item as an extra – a Pye radio.

At the Earls Court Show, the Frisky Sport was introduced to the public. The Frisky Sport was a soft-top powered by a 328cc Villiers engine. Although it was a four-wheeler, the rear track was substantially narrower than the front, there was no differential and it was fitted with a live rear axle. The car was both lively – with a top speed of 56mph – and economical with around 64mpg. Both of these performance figures were strong selling points.

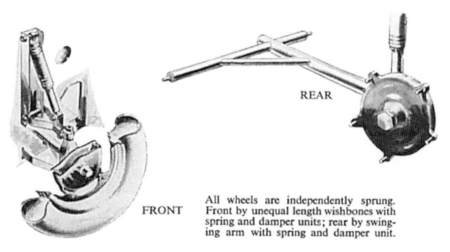

REAR

FRONT

All wheels are independently sprung. Front by unequal length wishbones with spring and damper units; rear by swinging arm with spring and damper unit.

The Berkeley T60 axles. Designers of pre-1939 cyclecars/microcars would have been stunned by the sophistication.

By the beginning of the 1960s the production of revivalist economy cars, previously known as cyclecars and then as microcars, came to a close. The Reliant Regal and Robin – cars made to car specifications – were three-wheelers. It was seemingly the end of the road for the cyclecar/microcar concept. Not so – currently the Piaggio Ape (pronounced 'apay', Italian for 'bee'), with a 50cc engine and four speeds with handlebar steering, shows that there is still a future for the cyclecar in the twentieth century. The cyclecar lives on.

The Peel P50, powered by a 50cc DKW moped engine, and capable of about 30mph. Reverse was simply a chromed handle bolted on to the fibreglass rear bumper.

The Frisky four wheel convertible, powered by a Villiers twin engine. Some models used an Excelsior Talisman Twin or Triple engine of 328 or 492cc.

The Meadows-designed Frisky had a fibreglass body and on hardtop models, engine access was via the passenger compartment.

The Frisky Family Three was a three wheeler version built to get round Britain's car licensing laws. This model has a full length Webasto roof.

FRISKY CAR CONTROL PLAN

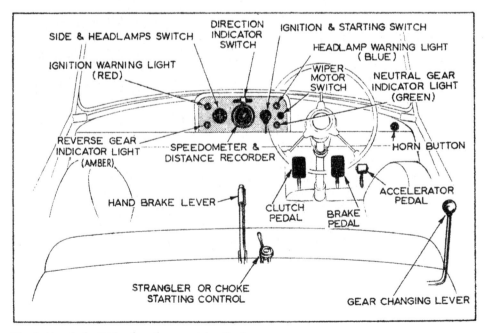

The dashboard of a Frisky, from the owner's handbook.

Forerunner of the Nobel was the Fuldamobil N2. Construction methods varied over the years and included aluminium over wood frame, fibreglass and a version of duroplast (as used on the Trabant).

The Nobel 200 was a british-built Fuldamobil. The Fuldamobil was sucessfully licensed to Chile, Sweden, the UK and Greece and construction lasted until 1969 when the supply of Heinkel engines ceased.

INTRODUCTION TO THE CAR

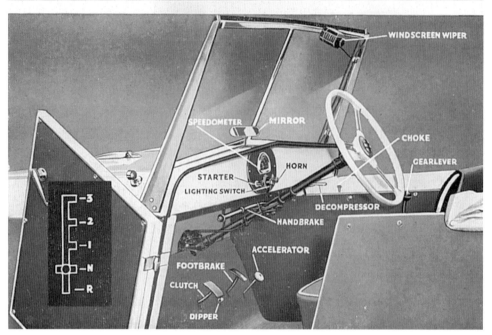

The controls of the Gordon, built by a branch of the Vernon's pools company. It was a ludicrously bad design with the engine overhanging the driver's side. Top speed, for the very brave or very foolish, was about 48mph.

The Gordon 8E/R with an 191cc, 8hp, Villiers 8E engine and fitted with electric starting and a reverse gear.

Charles Mochet was a designer and inventor of some note, having designed the velocycle as well as pre-war cyclecars. This is a CM175 from 1957.

One of the few Austrian microcars was the Felber. BMW also constructed some Isettas in Austria.

The Scootacar was manufactured in Leeds by Hunslet Engineering, perhaps more famous for their railway locomotives. It survived through three Marks, this one being a Mk1. It used a fan cooled Villiers 11E engine of 191cc and had a top speed of about 55mph.

The earliest Reliant vans were the same as its Raleigh predecessor, fitted with a vee twin JAP engine behind the steering head. This 1948 period 12cwt van used a development of the Austin 747cc engine. Sideways vision for the driver/navigator was limited.

One of the reasons that microcars did not survive in great numbers was their poor accident damage rate. Here is a Maico, having been hit by the Volkswagen on the right. The Maico, being a real car in miniature, could withstand the impact better than an Isetta or Messerschmitt.

A Brighton-built Isetta 300 Deluxe model of 1959 at the roadside. This view gives an idea of the limited luggage space of an Isetta. There was the rear parcel shelf above the engine, a small space under the seat and the floor in front of the passenger. An optional extra was a storage pocket on the inside of the front door.

The Lightburn Zeta was developed from the British-developed Astra in Australia and used a Villiers twin of 324cc. The very wide doors provided access to the rear as the back panel had no opening.

One man's collection of microcars. 'I am become as sounding brass,' Gordon Fitzgerald of Kendal. At the back is a 1962 BMW Isetta with a 300cc engine. The Peel P50 from the Isle of Man is a single-seater of 1964 with a 49cc DKW two stroke. The 1963 Trojan has a 200cc engine. At the front is a 1960 Kr200 Messerschmitt and a Heinkel. The Heinkel is the mother of the Trojan, except that the offspring has right-hand steering.

INDEX